Is There Life After Housework?

Don Aslett

Illustrated by Craig LaGory

Writer's Digest Books

Cincinnati, Ohio

First revised edition, 1981.
Second revised edition, 1982.
Second printing, October, 1982.
Third printing, December 1982.
Fourth printing, October 1983.
Fifth printing, March 1984.
Completely revised and expanded
edition, April 1985.
Second printing, September 1985.
Third printing, June 1986.
Fourth printing, March 1987.
Fifth printing, July 1987.

Library of Congress Cataloging in
Publication Data

Aslett, Don, 1935-
   Is there life after housework?
   Includes index.
   1. House cleaning. I. Title.
TX324.A76   648'.5   81-11666
ISBN 0-89879-165-0   AACR2

A *new edition of*
Life After Housework? . . .*Why?*

After cleaning I'd guess a million houses, I found myself giving talks on the subject. At the end of my first housecleaning "seminar," I felt a little like Elvis Presley—the women mobbed me. But all I did was share some of my professional secrets—tell and then show them how to take three hours of housework and do it in fifteen minutes.

To save the two hours of questions that stretched after every cleaning presentation after that, I wrote up a little pamphlet called "The Adventures of Betty Betterhouse" and handed copies out. There was a stampede in one auditorium when someone yelled, "There ain't gonna be enough to go around." I knew then that a bigger volume would be welcome, so I wrote a book and titled it *Is There Life After Housework?* Three major publishers turned me down, saying "Who's interested in housework?" So I went to a self-publishing class for a couple of days and then published the book myself, innocently printing up a tractor-trailer load of books. But that whole truckload—20,000—sold before I could get them into the bookstores.

Suddenly I found that a very alert and down-to-earth publisher (who luckily had a woman editor-in-chief and a general manager with six children) wanted my book. Promising me national publicity—that I'd actually get to clean a toilet or two on TV—Writer's Digest Books republished my book and it became a bestseller (in fact, for ten days it was ahead of *Joy of Sex* and *30 Days to a Beautiful Bottom*).

After a half-million copies had been sold and I had two other bestselling books on simplifying home chores under my belt, I discovered that I'd made a grave mistake in the first edition of *Is There Life After Housework?* I'd claimed I could save homemakers up to 75 percent of their cleaning time; that was wrong—I should have said "up to 80 percent." I wanted to have a massive recall like the automobile companies do and make the change; my publisher suggested a revision. So while I was at it I added some things I found my audience always wanted to know more about— about the principles of preventing housework, about wood floors, appliances, dusting, and painting. I put together better and more complete equipment and stain charts, and tossed in all sorts of little bits of information that as a thirty-year professional I had presumed everyone knew.

So we did it! And I think you'll like it.

Don A. Aslett

*You are entitled to a life of love,
fulfillment, and accomplishment, but
these rewards are almost impossible to
obtain when you spend your life
thrashing and wallowing in a muddle
of housework. Time—the time to love,
to be, to grow—is the most precious
commodity on earth. No one's time
should be wasted cleaning needlessly
or inefficiently.*

Table of Contents

1. A clean house: how does everyone else do it? 2
2. Is it organization or your energy level?........................10
3. Treasure sorting and storage strategy 20
4. What to expect from your husband and children 27
5. The old wives' tales: Ever hear these? 34
6. Relax and work less...48
7. Don't be caught streaking . . . windows........................55
8. Prevention—Keeping the enemy out.............................62
9. Floors under your foot and rule................................74
10. How to clean carpets for a softer life.........................86
11. What to do about furniture 106
12. Shorter visits to the bathroom 114
13. Success in high places.......................................120
14. Simplified wall and ceiling cleaning..........................126
15. Painting without fainting 138
16. Designing your own efficiency................................147
17. Why not be a professional housecleaner? 152
18. There *is* life after housework!..............................166

1.

A clean house

How does everyone else do it?

Most of us don't use any of these methods to clean our houses. We represent the 95 percent of homemakers who, often in a state of cobweb confusion at the end of the day, wonder, "Just how does everyone else do it?"

Every time we see another clean-and-organized success story, we end up depressed and frustrated. We try the miracle formulas, quick tips, and super systems, but when we find ourselves

Some lie. . . .
Some have mighty
lumpy rugs. . . .
Some have no
children. . . .
Some have a maid. . . .
Some browbeat their
husbands to do the
work. . . .
Some use only one
room in the house. . . .
Some never let anyone
in. . . .

still not progressing in the war against grime, grit, and grubbies, we again wonder why it works so well for others. "Something is surely wrong with me!" we conclude.

Newspaper columns, slick magazines, and bestselling authors have tried to provide all the answers for a "perfect home"—and have convinced too many homemakers they don't have a chance. This constant bombardment of get-clean-and-organized propaganda leaves millions of women wondering, "What's wrong with my system? Why am I the only one failing?"

Well, I don't think there's anything wrong with you or with any other woman struggling to run a home (and/or raise her kids, hold down a job, go back to school, do volunteer work). Housework is, for a fact, never-ending and little appreciated. There are no superwoman homemakers. Most women are barely managing, meeting daily crises and demands, just like you are, wondering too what's wrong with them. It's amazing that no real training is provided for the most complicated, life-affecting job on earth—homemaking.

The superwoman articles, books, and commercials are a failure if their intent is to inspire the homemaker to rise to maximum efficiency. Gimmicks, hints, formulas, and magic schedules for living happily ever after aren't the answer. Overestimating or underestimating your abilities in any situation feeds the monster of discouragement. When you're doing your best but see yourself falling short of your goals, it's hard to have a bright outlook or a sense of accomplishment.

Yet I assure you there are proven ways to have a clean house, and they don't hinge on magic, good luck, or genies in a cleaner jug. By learning how to *prevent* housework, and by using *professional* cleaning methods, you can reduce your household chore time by as much as 75 percent. You'll simply learn to clean more efficiently and effectively. My confidence in you and in this statement is anchored in thirty years as a professional housecleaner—and teaching and listening to thousands of women around the world talk about their cleaning.

A housecleaner is born

Fresh off the farm and unappreciative of my mother's labors to provide me with hearty meals, ironed shirts, and a clean bed, I found college life a far cry from a comfortable home. My appreciation for that home and mother became keener when I discovered how much of my time and money it took to support myself. For survival, I landed a job bottling pop for 75¢ an hour, my first non-farm job. The funds left after deductions were definitely not enough to get me through college. So I looked for a better-paying, part-time pastime.

Cleaning yards and houses seemed to be a likely prospect, and so my career as a world-renowned housecleaner was launched. Following afternoon classes, I'd suit up in a white uniform and knock on doors asking if I could assume some of the household drudgery. I received only a few sneers before I was snatched from the street and given a furnace-cleaning job, followed later by some floors, then some windows. On every job, the homemaker would watch and direct as I'd scrub, shovel, and polish. Next came wallpaper cleaning, wall washing, and cupboard cleaning. Word got out that there was an eager housecleaner loose in the neighborhood, and soon I had more work than I needed. I hired help, taught them what the homemakers had taught me—and the business grew. Carpet and upholstery cleaning were added to my list of skills.

Soon my business was a large one, in demand in towns outside the college city of Pocatello, Idaho.

Over the next ten years my unique housecleaning business received much public recognition—"College Boy Makes Good." Between newspaper headlines I acquired a vast amount of experience in housecleaning. I ruined grand piano tops, toppled china cabinets, broke windows, streaked walls, suffocated pet birds with ammonia, ruined murals, shrank wall-to-wall carpets into throw rugs, and pulled hundreds of other goofs. But with each job I got better, faster, and more efficient (at cleaning, not breaking). I cleaned log cabins with dirt floors and the plushest mansions in the country. Some days, with five housecleaning crews in operation, I'd clean several three-story homes from top to bottom.

But cleaning skill wasn't the only talent needed to run the company: Organization was important. All of us working in the business were full-time students, active in church and civic affairs, and the heads of large families.

My wife Barbara and I had six children in seven years. While operating the business, going to school, and getting a degree, I lettered three years in college athletics and was on the debating team. Because my co-workers and I had no alternative, we *had* to develop efficient methods to clean houses. Fortunately we received much opinionated coaching and direction from every homemaker we worked for.

In these years of "field experience" is based my confidence that I can show you how to attain greater housecleaning efficiency. Although I now serve as a consultant on building

efficiency and maintenance for the world's largest companies, I know that the homemaker faces some of the most difficult cleaning problems of all.

And to make the matter tougher, housework is something every woman is expected to do in addition to *homemaking*.

This is why I prefer to use the word "homemaker" rather than "housewife." "Housewife," like "janitor," has come to mean someone who slaves away at menial, boring work. The "home" in "homemaker" is important because home is the most personal, important place for us all. "Making" is a hint that the job can be creative and fun. Making a home a happy welcoming place means more to life than any high-powered industrial or office job.

The root of housework evil

Do you want to know what the biggest, ugliest housework problem is? It's that 90 percent of all housework is caused by men and children—and 90 percent of all housework is done by women. Like most men, I once viewed,

with a certain critical eye, my wife and other women struggling feverishly to get their housework finished. I ached to jump in and show those "disorganized gals" how an expert could square things away.

Soon the opportunity, along with a great lesson, came to me. Fresh out of college, I worked hard washing walls late at night to buy my wife a surprise plane ticket to Alaska. She was delighted to have her first flight ever and a chance to see her mother again. I bade her goodbye and told her to stay as many weeks as she wished, that I would care well for our six small children. (She wasted no time leaving, I assure you.) But my true thoughts were, "Now that I have her out of town, I'm going to shape up this disorganized house and make it as efficient as my business!"

I woke up at four the first morning and confidently mapped out the campaign of great household efficiency about to be enacted in our home. By 6:30 the kids were up, and they saluted before they went to the bathroom! By 7:30, the beds were made and the dishes were done and I was rolling to victory. We were putting the finishing touches on a new home, and my project for the day was constructing a vanity cabinet in the master bathroom—an easy half day's work. I had just started to glue the first board when "Waaa!" One of the kids had biffed another. I ran out and made peace, passed out the storybooks, and again picked up the hammer and board. "Waaa!"—someone cut a finger. Three Band-Aids and ten minutes of comforting and mercurochrome-dabbing later, I again picked up the hammer (after scraping off the now-dry glue) and had one nail started when "Waaa!"—a diaper to change (a cry that was repeated all day; I'd have sworn we had four in diapers at the same time).

Again I returned to work, and had started the second nail, when *ding-dong* (the milkman; I slammed the cottage cheese into the fridge), then *ding-dong* (the mailman; I ran down and signed for the package), then *ring-a-ling* (the school telephoning—Laura forgot her lunch money). Then *knock-knock*—"Can I borrow. . . ." Then *buzz*—time for lunch . . . *ding dong* . . . time for bottles. "Waaa!"—diapers again, etc., etc., etc. You would not believe how my morning went (or would you?). My building project looked like a chimpanzee special—dried glue and badly cut boards all over, and no real work accomplished. I discovered that dressing a kid once is just a warmup—one of those kids went through four outfits by 11:15. Noon came and another surprise—those little dudes don't appreciate what you do for them, all that work cooking and they threw food, slobbered, and not one of them thanked me. . . .

Nap time came, and would you believe little kids don't all go to sleep at the same time? I've bedded down 600 head of cattle easier and faster than those six kids. When I finally got them all down, no way was I going to hammer, play the stereo, or even turn a page loud and risk waking one of them! Fortunately, the day ended just before I did. I had two boards up on the cabinet by the time the last baby was read to sleep at midnight. The most famous housecleaner and best organizer in the West . . . had accomplished nothing! I was *so* tired and discouraged. The day before I'd bought five trucks, four people had asked me to lunch—I'd expanded my company into a new area—but that day, nothing!

The next morning, I again woke at four and again decided I was going to run things like my business. I'd change all the diapers ahead for the whole day! But it didn't work. Leaving out all the gory details of the next few days, my half-day cabinet job, only half-complete, bit the dust.

A week later my wife called to check on things. I pinched all the kids to get them howling in the background so I wouldn't have to beg her to come and save me. She did return at once, and I suddenly got efficient again.

Since this experience, my compassion, respect, and appreciation for the homemaker have grown considerably. I realized then for the first time how frustrating, time-consuming, and just plain hard the job of making a home is, and how much patience and ingenuity it takes.

In preparing this book I've tried to keep in mind the hundreds of other jobs the homemaker must perform simultaneously with housecleaning. Laundry, shopping, cooking, mending, and errands *ad infinitum* will always be required. Though housework can be shortened, and there *is* life after housework, life *during* housework must also go on.

This is why rigid cleaning methods and plans seldom work. Schedules and demands are different in every household, big houses are proportionately easier to clean than small ones, new houses are easier than old; so women trying to pattern their lives after others are eventually

disillusioned. . . . like the determined woman who tried a simple "foolproof" formula for keeping children from getting their dirty fingerprints all over the walls. She had read a "how to run a perfect home" article that advised, "Take Junior, sit him down and say, 'Junior, if you wash your hands three times a day, Mommy will give you a 25¢ raise in your allowance.'" Immediately the woman called her dirty-fingered son in and presented the proposal to him. "I promise," said the son. But the spots were still on the wall. The mother observed her son one morning, and indeed, he was keeping the bargain. He went to the sink, washed his hands and dried them, and repeated the procedure twice more. Then he left to play in the dirt.

It's frustrating to see commercial exaggerations of how well cleaning methods and materials work, especially when they're applied to a house in which everything is already perfect. You're not alone in being offended by the gorgeous TV housewife in expensive evening clothes who flips her pearls out of the way to mop the floor with Magic Glow. Occasionally an immaculate kid or two tiptoes past or a well-groomed dog ambles through the place, after which the "super-smelling clean-all," applied effortlessly, takes over. But don't be discouraged—there's something wrong with them, not you!

Miracle formulas, tricks, gimmicks, and solutions aren't the answer, and if they haven't worked for you, don't let it get you down, because they aren't the key to freedom from housework. The first principle of effective housework is not to have to do it! Being able to do it well is great, but it's greater not to have to do it at all. Your real goal is to *eliminate* all of it you can. In this book you'll learn how to get rid of a lot of it, and the rest I'll show you how to take care of quickly and efficiently.

Just remember that, while getting finished with any housework chore is a worthwhile goal, doing it in teeth-gritting agony is self-defeating. There are "have-to" jobs, no matter how good we are (like bathroom rings, fingerprints. . . .). You'll never escape them. But when you learn to minimize the time you spend on the have-to jobs, you'll finally be able to get to the "get-to" jobs, and they'll both become more pleasant, I promise! There *is* life after housework—and if you do it right, there can even be life *during* housework.

Once you start finding the extra time that once was all spent on housework, nothing in your home will be mediocre or dull. You'll rip down anything that's faded or ugly and replace it with the prettiest, most colorful, most refreshing things you can find or make. You'll throw out or trade

things that don't fit in. If something is torn or worn or forlorn, you'll look forward to taking care of it, not as a chore, but as a chance to better yourself and your home. You'll want to mend it, because it will be mending *you*. Once you have time, you'll be inspired to repair and refinish. The real struggle before wasn't the chore or item you had to service—it was the hopeless feeling that there was never any time for it. A lot of little things that need to be done really aren't work once you can get to them—and once you really believe that you can, you'll start looking forward to them! That's life *during* housework!

At the housecleaning seminars I've taught across the country, I've passed out thousands and thousands of registration cards with a space left for comments, special requests, or housecleaning wisdom. This was written on one: "I must tell you, I love to clean. I have a clean house and I've been using the same techniques you use for years now. Everything in my house looks good, but my husband accuses me of being lazy because I don't exhaust myself every day like his mother did. I make lots of handicrafts and things, and he can't get over the fact that everything is clean and yet I still have time to goof off. He is honestly upset. He thinks I have too much fun and don't work enough."

You can't win 'em all. You'll discover in your worrying about how other people do it that 90 percent of the time you're overestimating their results. Even in the cartoon world, Wonder Woman in all her glory never raised children, stabilized a husband, or cleaned and managed a house. Wonder Woman faced only criminals, not housework horrors.

You can be as much a Wonder

Woman as anyone you'll meet or read about, if you'll only learn to harness your own resources. Not many others are more efficient or have a neater house than you.

By following the simple secrets in this book, you'll become even more efficient, and will have more time to enjoy life after housework.

2.

Is it organization... or your energy level...

"I get the feeling at the end of every day that I haven't gotten anywhere and I'm never going to get anywhere. . . ." This is how a lovely young mother with a brand-new house and four small children rather concisely summed up a basic problem of homemaking: understanding what needs to be done but feeling that you lack the skill or direction to accomplish it. Even if you know what the rewards of the end result will be, constantly thinking you aren't getting there will discourage you and begin to prevent you from *wanting* to get there.

The big magic word

The big, magic word to homemakers, business managers—in fact, all of us—is *organization*. If we could just get ourselves properly organized, we could do anything (so we think). We spend a great deal of time trying to organize ourselves like the superwoman and superman formulas say we should, but still seem to get little accomplished. We subconsciously figure the "organizing" is going to do it for us.

This is wrong. There's no organization plan that supplies the answer or does the work. Is there hope? Yes, and this bit of good news will start this chapter off right— women are much better organizers than men. I say so, and if you ask any boss, school principal, or minister who organizes best, they'll agree with me: Women do! (If you want to prove it, send a man and woman to town, each with a list of things to do and get. The woman will be home in two hours with everything. Six hours later, the man will lumber in, only partly successful and mean as a bear.)

There is no one best way to organize

Organization is an ever-changing process; it's a journey, not a destination. Every minute of every day a new approach is being thought up. Everyone is different in temperament, attitude, build, energy, and ambition; every situation requires a different style of organization to get the job done. The secret isn't in how you get organized—it's in *wanting* to be organized and committing yourself to it. Once that's achieved, everything will fall into place. You can organize as well as anyone if you want to or have to. There isn't any "set" way to do anything. You don't have to eat the soup first or second in a meal—you can eat it last!

Your system of organization should fit you personally. It should be tailored to your style, your schedule, and your motivation. Some of us are day people; some, night. You run your own life— the clock doesn't run it.

Some organizational myths

I'm convinced that everyone can be organized if they have to be and if they quit trying to follow "know-it-all" methods and formulas. For example, some efficiency experts give this "foolproof" method of accomplishment.

They say, in essence, "Sit yourself down and make a list of the things you want to get done. Put the most important ones first. When you get up in the morning, start on the first one and don't leave it or go to the next one until the first is finished. Then go on to the second one and so on until you've finished with the list."

I can't imagine anyone being able to exist (let alone succeed) following that kind of organizational concept. It's grossly inefficient, noncreative, inflexible—not to mention no fun. For years I've worked closely with top executives from some of the world's largest corporations, and I've never met one who worked this way. Yet I know many homemakers who've been trying desperately to organize their lives to fit this ridiculous concept, and they are paying dearly for it, suffering endless frustration because they can't make it work for them. If I followed that style of organization in my business or personal activities, I'd be twenty years behind!

Look where trying to follow the 1-2-3-4 style of getting things done can lead you. Let's say you make a list of the following things to do this week (in addition to your regular chores):

1. Make the kids a birdhouse.
2. Water the garden.
3. Memorize my part of the poem for PTA play.
4. Send Grandmother a birthday card.
5. Get the new lawn in.

Enthusiastically, you tackle the five projects in the down-the-list style outlined by the efficiency experts. While in town, you pick up the birdhouse materials, and soon you get started on the house with full gusto; however, you forgot to get an adjustable bit to make the hole in the front of the birdhouse. So, at a critical point, you're stopped. The 1-2-3 track compels you to leave the task and take time out to secure the needed tool, which you do at a cost of twenty-three miles of driving and two hours of searching. You then paint an undercoat on the birdhouse, wait a day for it to dry, and then put the second coat on. After two days, task #1 is at last finished, so out to the garden next. You turn on the water. Four hours later the water is finally down the rows and task #2 is finished. Next you go into the house for a few hours to memorize the PTA poem, #3 on the list. Grandmother's card, item #4, you then pick up at the store, bring home, sign and address, and take to the post office. To put a hero's touch on #5, you pick up a book on lawns, work on the lawn for the last three days, and are finished with all your projects in one week!

Efficiency experts might have a week to spend to do all this, but you don't and neither do I. The tasks could easily be done in a day or more, of course, with a little margin for daydreaming on the side. How? By relying on your creativity and a more flexible system. While in town, before anything is started, pick up the card for Grandmother. While driving on to get the birdhouse materials, mentally build the house so you'll be aware of each thing that has to be picked up. While waiting for the lumberyard clerk to round up the materials, chat with one of the staff about lawn season and grass and at this time get the fertilizer, mulch, and seed for the anticipated lawn.

On the way home, turn off the car radio and start to memorize the PTA poem. Once you get home, lay out the materials for the birdhouse and build it. (Oops, we forgot the adjustable bit, too.) Let's stop the birdhouse immediately and go turn on the water for the garden, taking the poem with us to memorize while waiting for the water to get down the rows. Once the water is going, planting the lawn gets attention. Next, phone your brother-in-law, asking him to send his adjustable bit for the birdhouse home with your child who'll be coming by in a while from school. Continue to work on the lawn until you're too tired to hustle. After washing for supper, write out Grandmother's card so the children can take it to the mailbox on their way to school next morning. When your child arrives with the adjustable bit, drill the hole and paint the birdhouse. By this time, you're rested, so you tackle the lawn again. When tired—but finished with the lawn—you come in and give the birdhouse a second coat (you were smart enough to buy a fast-drying primer). By then it's late, but just time for another shot at the poem, and you've memorized it. Now all five things are completed in *one day* instead of a week, and look at the time you have left for yourself.

Impossible to do all that in one day? No. And you can apply this same principle to housework if you rely on your own skills and really want to get it done. Your freedom and ingenuity will produce creative energy. It's simply a matter of "multiple track"

organization. In housework, if you wait until one thing is completed before you start another—the single-track system—you'll take forever to finish and never get around to any freedom to enjoy life. Once you train yourself to the multiple-track method, thinking will be effortless. You'll just roll along accomplishing things. You won't have to drain your think tank or worry or sweat to organize. It will come naturally.

Here's the secret: The start and finish of a job are the difficult parts. So start the first project at once! As it gets rolling, begin the second. As the second gets in gear, attack the third.

By then the second one is done, so pounce on the fourth, fifth, and sixth, and if the third isn't done, start on the seventh. Don't start and finish any two tasks at the same time. Don't start one thing when you're finishing another. Start another project while you're in the middle of three or four, but don't start one at the end of another project. The multiple-track system is the right way to run many projects at the same time—and it's easy if you alternate starting and finishing times.

The way some women cook is a prime example of doing things the most efficient way. I've watched my grandmother, who had fifteen children, prepare eight different dishes for twelve people in just minutes—a miracle. But it wasn't a miracle—just good organization and the multiple-track system. She simply got eight things going at alternate times, nothing starting or ending at once. You've done that, haven't you, when you had to? No sense waiting for water to boil, biscuits to rise, salads to cool, lard to melt. She simply used the waiting time productively.

I've watched a one-track-system mother with one small child crumple in total frustration trying to manage her baby. Five years, a couple of sets of twins and two singles later, she's doing a marvelous job. How? She learned the four- or five-track organization system and applied it! Your mind is capable of it and your body is, too. The success of this system is amazing, and once you get it down, you'll benefit from it in every area of your life.

A large percentage of our housecleaning time is spent "putting out brush fires," as it's called in business. This simply means that if you take three seconds to close the gate behind you, you won't have to spend three days hunting for your dog. Many a housekeeper fails because all her efforts are spent taking care of problems that a little timely action would have prevented.

Homemakers are notorious for this. They spend twenty hours a year (and a lot of mental anguish) trying to remove felt-tip marker writing from walls, instead of a minute putting the pens out of reach of the kids; ten hours a year cleaning ovens or stovetops instead of fifteen minutes choosing a pot or pan that won't boil or slop over!

Simplicity vs. procrastination

A great deal of effort is expended as a result of failure to put out a simple timely effort. Here's a common everyday example: doing the dishes later instead of right after the meal. Notice how a simple chore multiples itself into an insurmountable obstacle of negative feeling and freedom-robbing discouragement. Do you take the time, over and over, to cope with an unsatisfactory situation instead of correcting the underlying problem?

Such as having to adjust the faucet handle just right so the drip is minimized, angling and massaging that sticky drawer for thirty seconds every time you use it to get it to slide back in, wondering and experimenting every time a fuse blows—which breaker switch is the lights, which is the heater, which is the outlet, which is the. . . . I think you know what I mean. (See the checklist at the end of this chapter.)

The best "organization" is simply deciding to do things before they get out of hand and dictate to *you* how and when they'll be done. Are you the slave or the master? Simplicity seldom goes hand in hand with procrastination. Do you clean up and put away things as soon as you're through (simplicity), or do you throw them in a pile to be rummaged through as they're needed (procrastination)? It only takes a few minutes to iron a blouse. Do you do it well ahead of the appointment, or five tense minutes before you have to dash out the door? (And of course then you have to take out and set up the ironing board for just one piece of clothing— and you risk scorching the blouse in your haste and having to find and iron another. . . .) Do you make your bed when you jump out (simplicity) or just before you go to bed again at night (procrastination)?

Do you fill out that speakers committee report when it's still fresh in your mind and will take only a few minutes, or do it when it's overdue? You've been strongly reminded to get it in, and now you'll spend hours doing so, because by now you've forgotten facts, mislaid evidence, and had to write an excuse letter.

The time lag between doing most things promptly and doing them late compounds and multiplies problems.

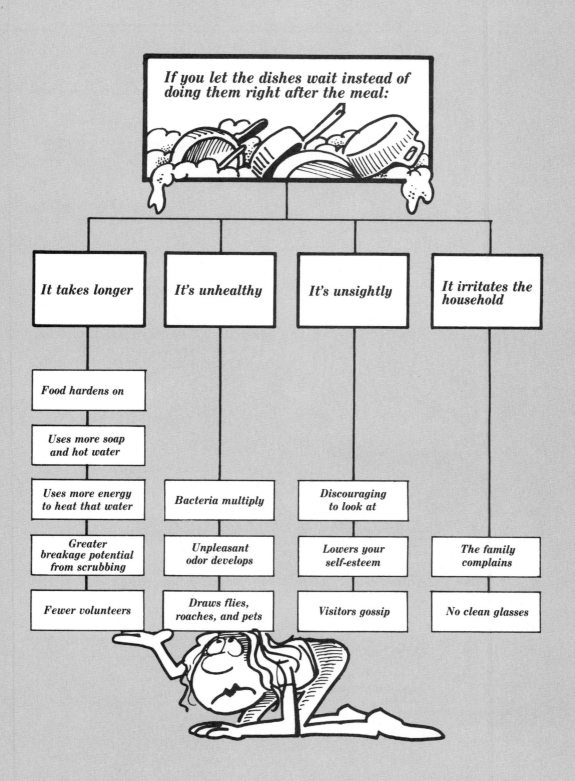

If you let the dishes wait instead of doing them right after the meal:

It takes longer

It's unhealthy

It's unsightly

It irritates the household

Food hardens on

Uses more soap and hot water

Uses more energy to heat that water

Bacteria multiply

Discouraging to look at

Greater breakage potential from scrubbing

Unpleasant odor develops

Lowers your self-esteem

The family complains

Fewer volunteers

Draws flies, roaches, and pets

Visitors gossip

No clean glasses

You end up spending time not simply getting the job done, but fighting and recovering from the problems created because you waited. Doing things when they take less time is not only good scheduling, it makes good sense: It will save energy and motivation to apply to more personally satisfying efforts than housework.

Most successful housekeepers clean in the morning. Cleaning at night shortchanges you on helpers, energy, light, and safety.

Back to the ever-growing list

Lists are great—as long as they don't run our lives. We all have our lists of things to do. I'd be lost without mine! We don't always *do* the things on the list, but they're always jotted down. At one time, my list grew to seventy-six "immediate" things to be done. It took all my time just to transfer the list to a new piece of paper when the old one wore out. If your list follows the typical pattern, at the bottom are the hard, unpleasant tasks, such as:

38. Tell Jack he's to be terminated.

39. Pour concrete for the back steps.

40. Go face the banker and get the loan.

41. Get my wisdom teeth pulled

42. Speak to George about taking a few more baths

or:

19. Clean the oven

20. Clean the 3-section storm windows

21. Volunteer to tend Dennis the Menace

22. Kick cousin Jack out of the front room

23. Go thru 700 old issues of Good Housekeeping

We have to be careful with that villain list. We're often so proud of ourselves for even writing something down on our list of things to be done that we immediately relax. We say to ourselves, "Boy, I'm glad I got that one started." After a few days we suddenly realize that nothing has been done, and we sneak a look at the list to see if that item has disappeared. It hasn't. We're so relieved to know that it wasn't forgotten, we leave it for a few more days. The day before the deadline, we've no choice but to face it, and generally get the item done in half the time we feared it would take!

A list has one big value and that's getting things recorded before you forget them. That's all! As for using a list to discipline yourself, forget it. *You have to do the things—the list won't do them for you.*

A schedule won't do them for you either. I dislike the regimentation of set schedules; they're only for inefficient people afraid they're going to run out of things to do. Some scheduling and budgeting of time is needed, but not to the extent that it dictates your every move and mood. You should run a schedule for your benefit, not the reverse. It can't be illustrated better than by a skit sent to me by homemaker Gladys Allen:

[Aslett arrives at the highly polished door of Mrs. Polly Programmed.]

Polly: *[Wearing a huge watch on her arm, feather duster in hand. She's groomed and dressed immaculately.] Hi, Mr. Aslett, won't you please take off your shoes and come in. [Dusts him off lightly as he removes his shoes.] How nice to have a visitor drop by. I have 6¼ minutes' relaxation time [checking her watch] before I have to knead the bread and water the alfalfa sprouts.*

Aslett: *Mrs. Programmed, I see that you're busy. . . . I just stopped by to invite you to a little efficiency seminar.*

Polly: *Nonsense! Now you come right here and sit down. I still have 5 minutes and 33 seconds of leisure time.*

Aslett: *[Sits down.] As you know, Mrs. P. . . .*

Polly: *[Interrupting] Oh, Mr. Aslett, would you mind sitting on this cushion? That one has already been sat on this morning. I like to alternate. The fabric wears much longer that way.*

Aslett: *[Moving to another cushion] Really? Now, I never would have thought of that.*

Polly: *My, yes! My last divan lasted seventy-eight days longer just by using that one little trick.*

Aslett: *What I've come to tell you, Mrs. Programmed, is that I've come up with a great new idea for a seminar, and I'd like to invite you to come preview it tomorrow morning at ten o'clock.*

Polly: *Ten o'clock Thursday? [Rushes to a big box labeled "Daily Schedules."] I've just typed up my schedules for the month. I'll have to check. [Pulls out a long folded sheet.]*

Aslett: *Is that your schedule for just one month?*

Polly: *One month? Oh, my no! This is my schedule for Thursday. [Studies it carefully, consults watch, makes a few changes with a pencil.] Now, what time did you say that would start tomorrow?*

Aslett: *10:00 a.m.*

Polly: *[Making a few more changes.] Yes, yes, I think I'll be able to work it in after all. If I get up at 5:00 a.m. instead of 6:00, I can have my laundry sorted and my scripture studies done by 7:00. I can get my drapes vacuumed and my children fed by 7:47. While they practice their violins, I can shine the furniture and wash the dishes. They leave for school at 8:19, which gives me just enough time to stir up a casserole for supper and get myself ready. Umm, yes. I should be able to leave here by 9:37 at the latest. By the way, Mr. Aslett, what did you say your seminar will be about?*

Aslett: *[Stands up with a sigh, shrugs weakly, unable to speak.]*

Highs and lows

The old up-and-down pattern is entrenched in our style of living—but how devastating it is to human feelings and efficient housekeeping! Most housecleaners unthinkingly roll along in this style. Once a week (or once a month) we clean the house, water the plants, and do everything just so, then we're "up." But immediately the spotlessness and satisfaction attained begin to erode as dust, spiders, children, animals, spouse, and guests mount their attack. It's frustrating because we've expended so much dedication and energy getting the house to its peak.

One elderly gentleman I met, recalling his mother's approach to housework, said, "She organized herself and the family so that all the housework (washing, ironing, baking, sewing, etc.) was done on Monday (one day, mind you). What an accomplishment! But she spent the other six days recovering to prepare for the big Monday cleanup again."

This kind of housecleaning approach gets old fast, and it gets you nowhere except an early grave. Even if your house is clean as often as it's dirty (50-50), you'll not be rewarded 50-50, because it's human nature to notice and respond to the negative, not the positive. Little is heard about the house if it's clean—but if it's dirty, everybody squawks, gossips, and complains. It's demoralizing, but you can't give up the battle. So you buckle down and restore your domain to order and cleanliness.

Now hold it. Now that you've got your house in top shape again, try something different.

A little consistency saves expending a lot of time, energy, and discouragement. Avoid the "up and down" style of housekeeping. Establish an *acceptable* cleanliness level and maintain it daily. If you really want to be freed from housework drudgery, this one change in style will work wonders for you. When you learn to keep house on a straight line, you'll not only find extra hours appearing, but some of the other up-and-down styles

you've been struggling with for years (exercising, cooking, letter writing, reading, gardening, etc.) will follow your housecleaning system and suddenly begin to be manageable. Your home will never stay static. It will be in a constant state of flux, if it's used as all homes should be. Avoid extremes both ways—too much polish is just as off-putting as too little. Gold-plating a house won't bring you anything but discouragement and worry.

To keep your home in a steady state of cleanliness and livability, you'll learn to wipe down shower walls and plumbing fixtures daily to avoid having to acid-bath hard water deposits monthly. You'll carry in a manageable armload of firewood whenever you enter the house, instead of spending a backbreaking hour lugging a week's worth in on Saturday. You'll wipe up spills immediately, when it's five times easier, faster, and much less damaging than putting it off.

You'll also discover that *eliminating* work does wonders for your efficiency. Try delegating, say, 60 percent of the daily chores to your family—you'll be amazed how much the need for picking up the house will decrease.

Do your big yearly cleaning each fall instead of spring; you'll marvel at how much longer the house stays looking nice. By cleaning *after* the open-window, kids-in-and-out-all-day season, you keep all that dust and pollen and dirt from deteriorating your house all winter—with the bonus that the house is cleaner for the winter holidays.

Remember to tie scheduling and organization to your own personal motivation or energy level. Add to that the conviction that what you have to do or want to do is really worth it, and organization will fall into place. You're a human being, not a machine. You don't start running at full efficiency the minute you're cranked up. If you try that, you're going to end up mighty discouraged. Don't work for a list or a schedule—fit everything to your physical, mental, or emotional state. By tying my energy level to production, I can knock out three magazine articles in an hour; I can't do one in eight hours when I have the drags. When I'm rolling, I tackle my most active and demanding work. When the drags invade, I file, sort, or do something that requires no creativity or mental energy. In both situations, I'm accomplishing a lot by fitting the task to my mood and personality.

Be yourself and decide what's most important to you. Wade into it during your best hours for that particular chore, and a miracle will happen. (You might end up writing a book on organization and selling it back to the supermen and -women of the world.)

3.

Treasure sorting & storage strategy

While cleaning a large, plush home during my junior year in college, I managed to wade through and clean a luxurious, treasure-laden bedroom and embarked on cleaning the closet. In addition to the expected arsenal of pricey wearing apparel, I had to move five exquisite cigarette lighters, forty-seven pairs of women's shoes (I kid you not), a case of 1920s *National Geographic*s, several tennis racquets, fourteen boxes of Christmas cards, six poodle collars, and numerous other items. It was a neat but completely stuffed closet, in harmony with the style of the woman who lived there. She was fifty-five years old, and possessed a handsome home decorated with elaborate art and delicate tapestries that she had spent part of her life collecting and the rest of her life cleaning and keeping track of. For thirty-five years, she had managed to keep her house clean and organized and all of her things dusted. This project of shuffling treasures around had taken her over half a lifetime.

Most of us are in the same condition as this owner of forty-seven pairs of shoes. Our treasures may not be expensive, but we have as many of them crammed in as many cubbyholes, which we shuffle through, sort and re-sort, climb over, worry about, and maintain for hours on end. What does it contribute to our lives or our personal edification? Even the Salvation Army store would label most of it JUNK. JUNK has frustrated more women than Robert Redford. JUNK has burned down more homes, caused more ulcers, and resulted in more arguments than can be imagined.

All for what reason? Accumulation? Sentiment? Security? Who knows?

The other 30 percent of the "things" that we have lying, kicking, and stored around may be of some worth to us. Small, important items left over from sewing, plumbing, playing, or a thousand other pastimes or projects can, at the right moment, be worth a hundred times their value. But remember, we're talking about 30 percent of what we have. Why own a houseful of useless objects that rob you of time and energy?

The burden of junk

It's amazing how we get ourselves into the junk habit. As the Law of the Packrat goes, "Junk will accumulate in proportion to the storage room available for it."

Before learning the shortcuts and professional methods of cleaning a house, we must first learn the art of "treasure sorting." This means differentiating between valuable and useless junk and promptly disposing of the latter. This is a job you can't palm off on anyone else, or postpone too long, because there's no escape from the toll that junk takes on your life. Everything stashed away or hidden—discreetly or indiscreetly—is also stashed in your mind and is subconsciously draining your mental energy. Once discarded, it's discarded from your mind, and you're free from keeping mental tabs on it.

Second homes often drain the people who can afford them. The owners maintain them mentally and physically for the entire year, yet only use them for a couple of weeks. If it were possible to calculate the emotions and affections, the caring and sharing energy that's silently burned up worrying about the home, it would surely outweigh the benefits of a couple of weeks or months spent occupying it.

Another burden junk thrusts on us is that we feel obligated to use it whether we need it or not. If we don't or can't use it, then we worry about why we have it at all! Junk will get you—don't sit there and argue that it won't.

The most valuable "someday useful" junk will stymie your emotional freedom if not handled properly. Inasmuch as all of us feel guilty and frustrated about our piles

of junk we have to eliminate the problem. In turn, it will eliminate an unbelievable amount of housework.

The origin of junk

There's a reason we quit using something: It's outdated, broken, unsafe, unattractive, or inoperable. This simply means that we don't need it any more—except, of course, for sentimental value. As each day goes by, it becomes more outdated, more unsafe, more unattractive, and will remain broken and inoperable. So learn to follow the 70-30 law that a magazine publisher made famous. He held up an

ordinary magazine and said, "Look, 70 percent of this magazine is advertising." So anyone who has any magazines or newspapers lying in boxes or piles around the house has up to 70 percent junk (depending on how healthy ad sales are). The first time you read a magazine, remove any article of interest to you and throw the 70 percent junk away. If you start doing this regularly, you'll rejoice for having eliminated those hernia-causing boxes of magazines (and besides, all those sculptured squash and hand-carved carrots we see in pictures were meant to be bronzed, not eaten!). Instead of piles of magazines, you'll have a thin, usable file of articles you want.

Other junk can be treated the same way. The faucet leaks and the handles are corroded, so we replace them with a sleek new chrome beauty. Looking at the old ones longingly, we can't bear to throw them away, because some day (even though they're broken, outdated, unattractive, and inoperable) we just might need a washer out of them. So we put them in the junk drawer or closet or shelf or hang them in the garage to get tangled up in the bicycle spokes. We could have removed the washers in two minutes and thrown the rest in the garbage, saving hours shuffling the old faucet around and dodging it. What a mighty grip junk has on us! We'll keep that worthless worn-out faucet for fifteen years, then in our move to Denver or Boston or Phoenix, into a new house, guess what we take with us . . . yes, the old faucet. We never know when we might need it. The average American moves fourteen times in a lifetime. If a third of your stuff is clutter, you could save eight moving van loads if you de-junked! People spend literally millions moving junk.

No matter how we may rationalize, "Oh well, we can put it in the attic" or "There's room in the basement," that junk should go to the dump. The number one secret of proper junk disposal or dispersal is to make the decision *at the time something is to be put away.* Because once you store it, sentimental attachment and mental obligation to use it (to justify the storage) begin to mount. And you'll never have time later to go back through all that stored stuff and decide.

Another good way to come to terms with junk is to face the fact of just how much room is really available for storage. If you can't conveniently store an item, then logically you cannot use it conveniently. And often the storage cost of an article is far higher than replacing it; it's not uncommon for people to pay $300 a year to rent a storage spot for $200 worth of stuff.

The economics of storage

On a special contract assignment at a Sun Valley resort one year, my company furnished decorated Christmas trees to the guests. The company that provided this service the year before lost $5,000 on the job, because they hired carpenters and highly paid laborers to put up, adorn, and take down the trees.

Hoping to improve efficiency, we enlisted local college kids and bought the decorations and trees wholesale. When the holiday season was over, our crew picked up the trees, took off the lights and metal stands, and packed and stored them for the next year's use. When it was totaled up, we lost

It's the "maybes" that get you!

only $900—an improvement, but still a deficit.

Then we did some "de-junking" thinking, and the following year made over $2,000 clear profit with half the headaches. Our secret? We just followed the basic rule of de-cluttering economy: When the Christmas holiday was over, instead of picking the trees up, undecorating them, accounting for all decorations and stands, and sorting, packing, and hauling everything to the storage warehouse, we just pitched the trees—tinsel, light bulbs, stands, and all—into the trash. The feeling of "waste" kept me awake for a while until I weighed it against the reality of the rewards. The savings on storage, energy, fuel, and labor were far more than we paid for the decorations!

But these things are valuable, you say? What about the value of the life and time to store, to clean, to insure, to transport, to protect—what does that cost? More than money: "Afford" is not simply a question of money, it's also an emotional and physical appraisal—what is the effect on your job, your physical being, your peace of mind? "Afford" is the capacity to absorb into your being, not your bank balance.

Think about the storage problem in your home. A lot of that stuff you're storing is useless. It's a constant source of worry. Most of it is unsafe, outdated, and ugly, so why keep it? Why spend a valuable part of yourself polishing, washing, dusting, and thinking about it? YOU CAN'T AFFORD JUNK. It will rob you physically, emotionally, and spiritually. Freeing yourself from junk will automatically free you from much of your housework (and it won't take any soap and water either); a cluttered house takes *much* more time and effort

to clean. You double your cleaning time by having to "pick up" a sloppy house, but even a neat house will take longer to clean than it ought to, if there's too much furniture or it's over-decorated.

Junk makes every job take longer

Clutter is one of the greatest enemies of efficiency and stealers of time—and that includes yours.

For every chore he tackles, the average person spends more time getting ready—hunting for a place, the tools, a reason to do it, etc.—than actually doing it. It takes only six seconds to drive a nail, often ten minutes to find the nails and hammer.

Junk makes every job harder and makes cleaning take forever. Any project we tackle, from building to disassembling, will be slowed, dampened, and diluted if we constantly have to fight our way to it in the midst of clutter.

If junk is taking up your good storage room it means you have to reach further and dig deeper to get the tool, book, suitcase, shirt, etc., you need. "Getting something out," instead of being a few-second job, often ends up a twenty-minute search-and-rescue mission.

If you'll just de-junk your home, the time you'll have left over in the course of a year will be enough to complete and pay for three credit hours in that night class you've always wanted to take. (When I say "de-junk," I don't mean sort your four cubbyholes of worthless stuff into three cubbyholes of worthless stuff!—or I'll tell on you!)

Now don't say "Oh, I know my junk has got to go, and one of these days, I'm going to. . . ." There are more reasons than housecleaning to de-junk your house (and your life). This might surprise you, but it's a reality: Many people are buried so deep in junk that their mates can't navigate the clutter to get to them. Your spouse can't give you attention and affection until he or she can find you. I've cleaned (or tried to clean) hundreds of homes where lonely, frustrated men and women, buried in junk, can't understand why they and their families aren't closer. Junk is the barrier! Junk (and junk projects and activities) prevents you from being free, available for affection or opportunity. Too often the things we save and store—for sentiment's sake or because they might be valuable some day—end up as tombstones for us. Boxes of mummified prom corsages and piles of corroded hubcaps will bury you but good. Get rid of your junk!

To start your de-junking program, begin with yourself! At an all-day seminar once I convinced the entire audience that junk is a universal problem, not the "other guy's." I gave every member of the audience two minutes to gather just the junk they were carrying with them (pockets—purses—briefcases), offering a prize for the most unique collection of junk (they initialed it for proper identification). My son passed around a large drawer and in minutes it overflowed. What did

I get, you wonder? (We all love other people's junk, don't we!) It was hilarious. It was all junk! Used flashbulbs, a 1976 calendar, old speeding tickets, partly eaten chocolate-covered peanuts, a hacksaw blade, a roll of toilet paper, two-year-old food coupons, rocks and pebbles, expired membership cards, half a pair of pantyhose, Christmas lists (after, not before!), broken compacts and empty lipstick containers, plus some censored items—and I suspect they held back plenty on me! The winning lady had a whole bulging hankyful . . . and she was the best-dressed person there! *Junk is a reality.*

If having piles, rooms, or buildings full of junk (even labeled "antique") is worth all those hours to shuffle it and all that mental energy to keep track of it, then unfortunately you value junk more than your time and freedom. (So much for those fantasies of being a happy, carefree vagabond.) If having a closet full of gleaming silver is worth hours of polishing time a month, you enjoy impressing people more than you value your time and your freedom. The storage strategy message is simple: Nothing exists in and of itself. Everything has a cost to acquire and to maintain. The majority of the cost you pay with your time and energy. Eliminate the junk and excess around your house. It's simple, and one of the easiest ways to free yourself from household imprisonment.

What to expect out of your husband and your children

On this subject I'll gladly assume the role of the learner. When you find something that works the miracle of getting husbands and children to take on their rightful share of the housework, let me know so I can tell the thousands of exasperated women I hear from every year.

This lack of cooperation from men and children is a grim reality, all right . . . but it doesn't have to be. While doing a consulting study for a large Eastern school district, I was introduced to a quiet grade school cafeteria. At the stroke of noon, 420 children converged enthusiastically on the polished lunchroom with trays and brown bags. Forty minutes later the room was quiet again, but not polished. It looked like a tornado had feasted instead of humans. Forks, food, and wrappers decorated the floor, the tables, chairs, walls, and even the light fixtures. When we were finishing the building tour *two hours* later, I noticed the janitor just finishing the cleaning. *Two 30-gallon garbage cans* were required to contain the mess the janitor picked up from that lunchroom.

The next day we were touring a similar school in town: same floor plan, same area, and 412 students. This time we arrived about fifteen minutes after lunch ended—and the place was immaculate! The janitor was scooping up what appeared to be the final dustpan of debris. I was told by the guide that not only was it the last dustpan, it was the *only* dustpan! This janitor had spent fifteen minutes restoring the room and filled only a small pan of dirt, while the janitor at the other school labored two hours in the same area, after the same number of children, and accumulated two garbage cans full. What was the difference? Same number of kids, same community, same size building— but . . . *not the same boss!*

It's not circumstance that causes you to have a messy house and spend two hours cleaning when you could spend fifteen minutes. It's you! The only difference between the schools was the principals. The first principal allowed the students freedom to eat and leave a mess; the other principal allowed the students the freedom of eating and simply added the responsibility of cleaning up their own mess. "Anything you mess up, you clean up" was the fair and simple rule. That meant crumbs, drops, and dribbles on tables, chairs, and floors. It took each kid seconds to perform the task and unquestionably taught and reinforced the most important ingredient of greatness: responsibility. Any woman who cleans up after a husband or a kid over two years old deserves the garbage cans she has to lug out every day!

I don't ordinarily suggest open rebellion or brute force, but I do offer these suggestions:

1. Refuse to be the janitor for the kids' and husband's messes. Picking up after them is bad for everyone involved. You teach irresponsibility perfectly when you assume someone else's responsibility (except those who don't know any better or can't help themselves). Insist that everyone clean up his or her own messes and premises: If they're old enough to mess up, they're old enough to clean up!

2. Write down and post needs. When you ask for (or demand) help, most family members will begin to assist you. Written messages

eliminate short memories and the innocent phrase "I didn't know you needed anything done."

3. *Make it easy for them to help.* To encourage bed-making, for instance, use one heavy blanket instead of several thinner ones (better yet, invest in European-style comforters that serve as blanket and bedspread). Teach the kids to spread the sheet and blanket and then circle the bed once, tucking as they go.

Make sure everyone has plenty of bins and hangers for personal belongings and the house will be tidier.

4. *Be patient. Be persistent. Use praise lavishly when it's deserved. Appeal to their vanity (this may work especially well on a husband). Remember, you can catch more flies with honey than with vinegar.*

5. *Leave home or play sick, if necessary.*

Sorry I can't help you more on this one! Just remember—it's as much for your husband's and kids' good as it is for you. So stand your ground!

P.S. My apologies to the 5 percent of husbands and children who already do their share around the house.

5.

The old wives tales

Ever hear these?

"Never shampoo carpets when they're new; they get dirty faster."

"Toothpaste and peanut butter remove black marks."

"Start washing from the bottom of the wall and work up."

"Use newspaper to polish your windows."

"Dried bread crumbs clean wallpaper."

Some of these might possibly work, but why go the long way around to get the job done? Spring isn't the best time to clean indoors—late fall is. Who wants to be cooped up with paint and ammonia fumes when springtime blossoms are fragrant? Painting isn't cheaper than cleaning; cleaning averages 60 to 70 percent less. Carpets don't get dirty faster after the first shampooing, if you do it right. Newspapers aren't good for polishing (only for training puppies and peeks at the funnies). Toothpaste and peanut butter do remove marks because they're abrasive—but they also cut the gloss of good enamel paint, and the resulting dull patch looks worse than the original mark.

For centuries, "secrets" of sure-cleaning brews have been passed on to young housekeepers. These formulas are applied unsuccessfully, yet on deathbeds are whispered to the next generation. Hence, even in this day of modern science, well-educated homemakers living in up-to-the-minute homes are still using powdered frogs' legs to remove inkstains from their carpets and crumbled cottage cheese to polish brass doorknobs.

I have yet to find a magic cleaner or solution that will take all the work out of cleaning a house. Less than 2 percent of the hundreds of old wives' tales sent or repeated to me even *worked*. And there's no magic in the bottle, either. The "cleaning cyclone" that whips out of the container isn't interested in cleaning for you when it's getting $150,000 for a minute on TV. Even if that solution—or any solution—is as good as advertisers say it is, it will have little effect on your cleaning time.

It's not what you clean with so much as how you go about it that really matters. So forget most of the old wives' tales you've heard and commercials you've seen and follow some simple professional methods that have been used efficiently and safely for decades.

Whatever you do, don't feel it your patriotic or economic duty to mix up your own money-saving brew. Some of the results are ridiculous. For example, it's easy to make your own glue, isn't it? Just find an old cow, kill it, and cut off as many hooves as you need for as much glue as you want. Grind them up in your trusty blender, then add. . . .

It's not worth it when you can spend 89¢ and get something better. Besides, it's cheaper than finding a cow and not nearly as messy as killing one.

Homemakers trying to make their own home brew furniture polish can spend three hours rounding up the materials and mixing up a solution that costs $5.45 for ingredients alone—instead of buying a commercial polish for $2.49 that's tested, safe, and guaranteed not to rot, explode, or poison. Remember, **it's your time that's valuable.** A half-century of professional cleaners' records show that out of every dollar spent for cleaning, only 5½¢ is for supplies and equipment; almost the same ratio holds true in the home. Your time and safety are the valuable commodities, not the supplies.

Most home brews are misguided formulations. For instance, most homemade furniture polishes call for linseed oil—a penetrant that conditions raw wood but that, when smeared on *finished* wood (which most furniture is), acts as a sticky magnet to every passing speck of dust. Many homemakers pour chlorine bleach into everything from mop water to toilet bowls, to no avail—bleach is an oxidizing agent that doesn't clean a thing. And don't spend your precious hours grinding and rubbing trying to get vinegar to perform like soap. Vinegar isn't a cleaner, it's a rinsing agent. The "squeak" is what turns you on!

Figuring this from a "free me from housework" angle, using good, efficient—even expensive—supplies and equipment is a cheap way to go if it cuts your time down. For example, if you pay $50 for a gallon of wax, it's a wise buy if it means that whatever you apply it to will only need annual or biennial cleaning and waxing.

Your household tools are your power tools

A gross injustice is usually inflicted on women in this area. Over and over, I see homemakers using an old rattletrap vacuum hardly capable of running, let alone sucking up any dirt. The hose is full of holes, the cord is worn and offers instant electrocution if touched in the wrong place. Every day women wrestle with these machines to do the housework, while in basements and garages sit $400 radial-arm saws and other power tools their husbands don't use or haven't used in six months! Men need these macho tools to give their masculinity an occasional boost—while women fight unsafe, ineffective vacuums for hours . . . every day! Husbands' closets are full of expensive toys that they use one or two days a year, while their wives are cooking three square meals on an electric stove with worn-out switches, or bunching tricot on a twenty-year-old single-stitch sewing machine . . . daily! The kitchen junk drawer (you know, that drawer with all the parts, spare tools, lids, screws, handles, matches, nails, etc.) is used more by the average man than his $800 solid oak workbench.

In most cases, after an industrious project or two, men seldom use their expensive tools; as investments go, such tools are poor ones. Time is our most valuable commodity, and good housecleaning tools and equipment can save hundreds of hours a year.

My wife the bread mixer

A confident husband pulled up in front of a specialty shop, parked his $33,000 Mercedes carefully, and strolled into the store. He paused to examine a new bread mixer, advertised to cut breadmaking time dramatically. The clerk eased up to him and politely suggested, "Why don't you buy a bread mixer for your wife?" "Ha!" said the man triumphantly, "Why should I buy one? I *married* a bread mixer."

This kind of attitude is an unimaginable infringement of one individual upon another. Men are the greatest offenders because traditionally a man's time has been considered to be of greater value. Tradition has validity, but not here. No one's time is worth more or less than another's; for a human being time is to love, to feel, to be, to experience, to serve, to relax, or to edify self. Position, sex, status, age, etc., have no bearing on the matter. Too many men think that they married a "bread mixer," maid, taxi driver, gardener, nurse, washerwoman— forgetting that their mate is entitled to the same share of "time" that they are. The average man reacts almost violently when his wife quietly asks for a $75 pressure cooker to make her more efficient in the kitchen and provide better nutrition for the family.

The same man will slap a $149 telescopic sight on his rifle (used once a year at hunting time) and never even bother to mention it to his wife.

On this earth, no one's time is worth any more than anyone else's. I used to send my wife to town or on errands to do "the piddly things" because my time was worth "so much"—after all, I could get $50 to $100 an hour for consulting jobs. I was way off base. Any woman's time is worth what any man's is.

Time—calculated in terms of the ability to appreciate and to experience—is of equal value to all human beings.

Homeowners should take a serious look around their houses. The tools likely to be used most and those capable of saving the most time are the ones to purchase. Anything that can be purchased to save time in housework is just as important as a new computer for the business! Buy up! (And don't spend all the money on little-used and often useless "trinket" attachments to cleaning machines or appliances; concentrate on solid basic tools and supplies.)

What's a homemaker to do?

If you can read, you can forget the witch potions and the glamorously packaged, overpriced household cleaners you've been using. The Yellow Pages in almost every phone directory in the world list janitorial supply firms. These are (generally) wholesale outlets where commercial cleaning companies buy many of their supplies. It's here you'll find the items I refer to in this book that can't be bought at the supermarket or hardware store. The rest professionals buy at a local supermarket, same as you do. The prices at janitorial supply houses vary, but I've never run into one in the multistate area where I've cleaned that wouldn't sell to a homemaker.

Wholesale or retail? Well, you can get either price. And either is better than the price of comparable supplies at the supermarket. The best way to try for wholesale price is to walk in with dignity and authority, squinting confidently at the shelves of cleaning material and equipment (few of which you'll recognize the first time), and say, "I'm Mrs. Van Snoot of Snoot, Snoot, Frisky, and Melvin (you, your husband, cat, and dog; the more you sound like a law firm, the better). I need one gallon of metal interlock self-polishing floor finish." This usually convinces the seller that you're official, and he or she will generally offer you the contractor's price, since most suppliers are great people and run "hungry" establishments. If the supplier asks you a question like, "Do you want polymer or carnauba base?" don't lose your nerve. Just say,

Give me the house's best-selling brand.

(Forty janitor companies can't be wrong!) I'm sure if you don't get the contractor's price, you'll at least get a discount.

Store the bulk of your cleaning equipment and supplies in a convenient central location. Keep a few frequently used supplies where you use them—a spray bottle of disinfectant should stay in the bathroom.

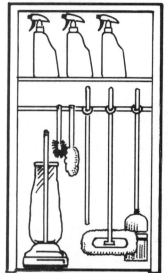

Most cleaning jobs require only a few basic professional supplies.

Store your supplies simply and safely!

Which supplies to use: where and when?

I'll discuss these as we cover each area of cleaning. Just remember this: There's no magic in the bottle or machine. The basics of effective cleaning are extremely simple, and you need just a few professional supplies. A chart at the end of this chapter lists the basic professional tools you'll find useful. A home will be well prepared for efficient cleaning and maintenance if it's equipped with the items listed. (If you can't find them, write me and I'll send you a mail-order catalog.)

Proper supplies— big returns

There are more benefits from using the right equipment and supplies than merely doing a (1) faster and (2) better job. There are: (3) safety—you'll be using fewer, simpler items that will be safer to use and easier to store out of children's reach; (4) cost—in the long run you'll spend a lot less on cleaning supplies if you select and use them properly; (5) depreciation—using proper cleaning supplies and tools reduces damage to and deterioration of the surfaces and structures you're cleaning; (6) storage—fewer and more efficient concentrated supplies take up less of the storage space you probably don't have enough of anyway.

If your cleaning closet is full of fancy cans and bottles—Zippo, Rippo, Snort, Rubb Off, Scale Off, Goof Off— I promise a roomier closet when you learn the secrets of proper cleaning.

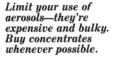

Limit your use of aerosols—they're expensive and bulky. Buy concentrates whenever possible.

Many of those chemicals and cleaners crammed into every cupboard and under every sink aren't all that effective. They use up valuable storage room, they're safety hazards for children, and many of them actually damage household surfaces.

Most homemakers' cleaner storage areas (under the sink, the pantry, the closet) look like Tom Edison's chemical cache just seconds before the explosion. Many of these things simply get wasted—we have so many, we forget to use them.

Canned expense

The aerosol can has pressured itself into the lives of all. Toothpaste, hair spray, deodorizers, even cheese food—just about everything comes in aerosol because we've been convinced it takes too much effort to do any more than push a button. We've carried this principle over into our housecleaning systems, paying dollars for pennies' worth of cleaners and compressed gas.

Concentrates are 80 percent cheaper than ordinary "household cleaning" products. They take a lot less room to store, and, because they're professional products, they do a better job.

Some cleaner concentrates come in small packets pre-measured for use in a bucket or spray bottle. Mix the concentrate with water as directed on the label.

Some aerosols are convenient enough to justify buying them, but for the most part, they're so bulky and expensive you don't get your money's worth in mileage or quality.

To replace most of the aerosols you now use, go to the janitorial house and buy four or five reusable commercial plastic spray bottles. Buy your chemicals, cleaners, and disinfectants concentrated, in gallons, or in the handy pre-measured superconcentrate packets. Mix them with water at the suggested dilution ratios and put the solutions in spray bottles. Label the bottles with a waterproof marker or make sure each chemical is a different color, lest you end up cleaning windows with upholstery shampoo. These plastic spray bottles are unbreakable, durable, won't nick cupboards, and are extremely efficient and economical to use, whether for heavy-duty cleaning or smaller "keep up" jobs.

For most general cleaning purposes and "keep up" cleaning, use a 1-quart spray bottle. Just add concentrate to water according to directions. This works well for spot cleaning many different surfaces.

You need only four basic cleaners

1. NEUTRAL CLEANER: Can be used for almost any type of cleaning. Won't damage surfaces—even wood—because it's pH neutral, neither acid nor alkaline.

2. DISINFECTANT CLEANER: For bathrooms and other areas needing germicidal action. Buy only a quaternary neutral type—it's nontoxic and won't damage most surfaces.

3. COMMERCIAL WAX STRIPPER/DEGREASER: For removing wax and for tough cleaning jobs where grease is a problem.

4. EVAPORATING ALCOHOL-BASED CLEANER: For cleaning small windows, polishing mirrors, appliances, tiles, etc.

When using any kind of cleaner, commercial or household, *read the label.* Don't sniff (and for heaven's sake, don't taste) to see what's in the jug; a rose will never smell the same if you ever get a strong whiff from a commercial ammonia bottle. And be sure to dilute cleaners properly. Our tendency is to say, "If a little does a good job, a lot will do better." This is as silly as saying, "If a teaspoon of baking powder will make the biscuits rise, then a cup should do wonders." We often gluggy-glug-glug too much soap into the water and actually destroy the chemical's dirt-suspending and grease-cutting action. Read the directions before pouring. Remember, you don't clean alone. You have two helpers, water and chemicals; they'll do most of the work.

"Miracle" solutions and "magic" tools aren't the only carryover from old wives' tales. Household advice columns are everywhere in newspapers and magazines. "Helpful hints" often only help add frustration. In a recent "Forty Ways to Save Time in the Home" article, I found only one tip that was unquestionably beneficial. Be discerning, check sources, and use your head in choosing housecleaning "advice."

You can get by without advice like "Buy a second vacuum cleaner for upstairs" or "Color-coordinate all your bathrooms so the towels will match and you'll always be ready for unexpected company." What you need to learn most of all is how to choose and use supplies and materials so as to use fewer hours of your time to have a cleaner home than you've ever had before. I'll explain how to accomplish this as we cover each major cleaning area in detail.

By the way—did you know that a paste of strawberries, wheat germ, ground glass, and baking soda will polish the bottom of a Boy Scout's cooking kit? (But so will a 2¢ scouring pad!)

Professional Equipment & Supplies

ITEM	SIZE TYPE	USE	SOURCE
CLEANING CLOTH	made from 9"x18" piece of cotton terrycloth	Replaces the "rag." Can be used for most cleaning jobs; especially effective in wall and ceiling cleaning. Folding and turning inside out provides 16 cleaning surfaces. (See Chapter 14 for details on how to make and use a cleaning cloth.)	homemade
MASSLINN CLOTH ✱	11"x17", disposable	For dusting. The specially treated paper "cloth" collects dust instead of scattering it. Leaves soft sheen on furniture, doesn't create buildup.	janitorial supply house
LAMBSWOOL DUSTER ✱	lambswool or synthetic puff on 24" or 30" handle	Picks up dust by static attraction. Extremely useful for high dusting, picture frames, moldings, blinds, books, cobwebs, houseplants, etc.	janitorial supply house or discount store
CELLULOSE SPONGE	various sizes, 4"x6"x1½" is a handy size.	For any washing or absorbing job. You can cut sponge to fit your hand. Always squeeze, never wring.	discount store or paint store
SCRUBBING SPONGE ✱	two-layer nylon and cellulose	Use where limited abrasion is needed. Use the type with a white nylon side on fixtures, sinks, showers, etc. Always wet before using. Good in the bathroom and kitchen. The slightly larger scrubbing sponges with a harsher green nylon side should only be used on nondamageable surfaces— not on enamel, porcelain, or stainless steel.	discount store or supermarket
SPRAY BOTTLE ✱	1 pt. or 1 qt. plastic trigger spray	To fill with diluted concentrated cleaners for hand spray work on spots, bathrooms, windows, or other small cleaning duties. Keep several around the house in convenient locations.	janitorial supply house or discount store

DRY SPONGE *	5"x7"x½" treated or natural rubber	(Don's favorite cleaning tool.) Use on flat-painted walls and ceilings, wallpaper, lampshades, oil paintings. Cleans many surfaces better, faster, and less messily than liquid cleaners. Discard when dirt-saturated.	paint store or janitorial supply store
WINDOW SQUEEGEE*	10", 12", or 14" Brass frame, rubber blade. Ettore Steccone is a good brand.	Strictly for window cleaning. Avoid contact with rough surfaces so rubber blade will stay perfectly sharp. Fits extension handle (see Optional Equipment Chart).	janitorial supply house
DUST MOP*	12" or 14" cotton head, rotating handle	For use on all hard floors. Fast and efficient; lasts for years. Use dust treatment (see p. 83) for best results. Shake out and vacuum head regularly; launder when dirt-saturated, then re-treat.	janitorial supply house
SPONGE MOP	various sizes Squeeze handle, changeable head	For damp-mopping in homes with a small amount of hard flooring. Can also be used to apply wax to floors.	discount store or supermarket
HAND FLOOR SCRUBBER *	hand tool with 5"x10" nylon pad	Also called a Scrubbee Doo. For scrubbing hard floors. Especially effective for scrubbing edges. Don wouldn't trade his for a gold-plated floor machine. The holder comes prepacked with pads.	janitorial supply house

For your convenience, those items marked * are available by mail. For more information and a free catalog write to: HOUSEWORK INC., P.O. Box 39, Pocatello, ID 83204.

The cleaning compounds described in this chart and elsewhere in this book are no more dangerous than many preparations found on supermarket shelves. But since most janitorial supplies do not come with child-proof lids, be sure to keep them out of the reach of children.

FLOOR SQUEEGEE*	18" push-pull Ettore Steccone is a good brand	Floor cleaning, picking up water, drying sidewalks and garage floors. Use instead of a slop mop when stripping or refinishing a hard floor. See Chapter 9 for detailed instructions on using a floor squeegee when stripping a floor.	janitorial supply house
BOWL SWAB*	3" heavy-duty cotton or rayon	Enables you to use bowl cleaner neatly and safely. Swab is used to force water out of toilet bowl (see p. 118), soaked with bowl cleaner, then swabbed around interior of bowl.	janitorial supply house
MATS (indoor and outdoor)*	3'x4'; 3'x5', or 3'x6'—nylon or olefin fiber on vinyl or rubber backing. Available in a wide range of colors.	Helps remove dust, grit, and other debris from shoes. Absorb mud and water from foot traffic.	janitorial supply house
UPRIGHT VACUUM*	12" 6 amp commercial beater-brush model with cloth bag. Don't buy half a dozen attachments; get a long cord.	For carpet and rug vacuuming.	janitorial supply house
WET-DRY VACUUM	5-gallon metal or plastic tank. Get squeegee, upholstery, and edge tool attachments with it.	Used for all household vacuuming, to pick up water when scrubbing floor, to pick up spills and overflows. Be sure you get one with a rust resistant tank and side hose attachments.	discount store; janitorial supply house

HEAVY DUTY NEUTRAL CLEANER*	concentrate—gallon or packet size	Dilute as directed for mopping, spray cleaning, cleaning painted surfaces, paneling, and all general cleaning where a disinfectant isn't needed. Also for removing fingerprints from furniture and walls—won't damage surfaces.	janitorial supply house
DISINFECTANT CLEANER*	quaternary type concentrate—gallon or packet size	Dilute as directed for use in bathroom cleaning or mopping and wherever else sanitation is essential.	janitorial supply house
ALCOHOL-BASED GLASS CLEANER*	concentrate—gallon or packet size	Dilute as directed to clean mirrors, small windows, appliances, chrome, etc.	janitorial supply house
COMMERCIAL WAX STRIPPER/ DEGREASER*	1 gallon, ammoniated or non-ammoniated	For removing wax from hard flooring. And tough cleaning jobs where grease is a problem (vent fans, top of refrigerator, etc.).	janitorial supply house
FLOOR WAX*	1 gallon or packet size, metal interlock self-polishing	To protect all hard floor surfaces— wood, tile, linoleum, sealed concrete, and no-wax floors.	janitorial supply house
NATURAL WOOD OIL SOAP*	organic—vegetable oil	Cleans and leaves a soft sheen on wood furniture, paneling, etc.	discount store or supermarket

Optional Professional Equipment

ITEM	SIZE TYPE	USE	SOURCE
EXTENSION HANDLE ✳	4'-8' metal, rubber handle	Lightweight, easy to use. Extends from 4 to 8 feet to safely reach high places. Fits squeegee, Golden Glove window washer, roller brushes, etc.	janitorial supply house
GOLDEN GLOVE WINDOW WASHER ✳	10" or 12" aluminum holder with fabric head	Use to apply cleaning solution to windows prior to squeegeeing. Great for high windows and high dusting. Fits extension handle.	janitorial supply house
WET MOP	16 oz. rayon layflat	For use if you have a great deal of hard flooring. Screw type handle enables heads to be replaced easily.	janitorial supply house
MOP BUCKET	18-qt. metal or plastic with self-contained roller wringer.	If you wet-mop, the self-contained roller saves hand injuries from hand-wringing. Use for mopping, wall washing, mixing, and as a punchbowl at a janitor's wedding.	janitorial supply house

PUMICE STONE ✱	small bar or block of pumice	To remove accumulated hard water ring in toilet. (Not for use on tubs, bold-colored fixtures, or tile.)	janitorial supply house
PHOSPHORIC ACID CLEANER ✱	quart	To remove mineral deposits from tile and fixtures.	janitorial supply house
SCOTCHGARD	aerosol or bulk	Soil-retarding treatment for upholstery and carpets.	janitorial supply house, discount store, or supermarket
NYLON-BRISTLED SCRUB BRUSH	varies	For cleaning textured or easily damaged items such as screens and blinds.	discount store or supermarket
BONNET MACHINE	uses 6"-13" cotton pads	Wet with recommended cleaning solution, wring, and place under floor machine to "buff" surface dirt off carpets. A carpet maintenance program that saves money, time, and your carpet.	janitorial supply house

6.

Relax & work less

A big event was coming to a small town and in preparation, the townspeople resolved to clean the hardwood floor in the village recreation center. They decided to scrub all the dirt and old wax buildup from the floor and apply a new coat of varnish. The committee in charge chose four of the best housecleaners and some husbands and the building janitor to do the job.

It took the group of seven most of a Saturday to finish it. Six hours they labored, spending a total of forty-two hours to get the floor ready for the finish application.

Four years later, after much hard use, the floor again needed the same attention. I had a free day, and since I enjoy cleaning floors, I volunteered to do the job at no charge. I refused the help of other volunteering townspeople and the janitor and instead used my sons, who were twelve and eight years old. We showed up at the building at 10:30 and went home early for lunch at 11:45. The job was completed perfectly in 1¼ hours, or for the three of us 3¾ total hours, much less than the 42 hours used by the group. We used three fewer mops, half the cleaners and strippers, and a tenth the hot water—and did a much better job.

I'm not any faster a worker than most of you, nor did I have any secret tools. Any of you could have done the same thing, using a valuable principle of cleaning: Relax and work less. To relate this principle more directly to the domestic front, let's take a glimpse of Betty Betterhouse in action.

It's been an unbelievable morning. In addition to her own seven children, fourteen friends and relatives, caught in a snowstorm, were overnight guests in her home. They consumed dozens of whole-wheat pancakes, eggs, and other breakfast goodies. It was two hours before Betty finally saw her unexpected guests depart and the children off to school. She then turned to the task of restoring her kitchen to livable condition. The drops of batter, jam, and grease covering her stove and countertop were now hard and dry. Betty began scrubbing one end of the counter furiously. Finally loosening (or wearing away) the spattered batter in one spot, she'd move on another few inches to grind some more of the droplets away. Fifteen minutes of exhausting effort later, she had the counter presentable.

Eliminate— Saturate— Dissolve— Remove

Betty could have saved more than ten minutes and at the same time been easier on the countertop surface if she had used the cleaning principle my sons and I used on the floor. You could call it the universal law of cleaning: Eliminate—saturate—dissolve— remove. You can do 75 percent of your cleaning with your head, not your hands—because 75 percent of soil removal is done chemically, not by elbow grease. Scrubbing to clean something went out with beating your clothes on a rock by the riverside. Betty needs only to sweep all the loose food particles from the countertop (*eliminate*: 15 seconds). She should then soak her dishcloth in soapy water and generously wet the entire area (*saturate:* 15 seconds), giving the liquid a few minutes to soak and loosen the spatters (*dissolve*). Then she merely has to wipe the mushy residue off (*remove*). Just a few minutes for the total job.

Of course, many of us have been doing this for years, not only on our countertops, but on appliances, floors, walls, sinks, tubs, shower stalls, automobiles, and 400 other places that might have used Betty's old time-consuming system. Hard soap crust on the bathroom sink where the hand soap sits can take several minutes of scrubbing, but if it were sprayed or dampened first, it could be wiped off in seconds. Almost everything will clean *itself* with water and the right chemical. Water is practically free and with a few cents' worth of chemicals it can replace numerous hours of your time if used according to the principle outlined above. It's incredibly easy to apply the right solution and wait. Leave. Read. Rest! Apply more solution in another area, or do anything you want while the solution's chemical action loosens and suspends the dirt. Unless you get your kicks out of scrubbing, there's not much reason to scrape and grind soil off.

I've watched people try to clean the grease and dust settled on top of their fridge. They wipe the cleaning solution on—and before it has time to break the gunk down and release it from the surface, they start scrubbing furiously. Let the solution do the work! By using the simple principle of

eliminate—saturate—dissolve—remove in all cleaning, you can cut time and energy expenditure as much as we cut the floor job for the town recreation center.

On your house floors, for example, remove the large obvious objects (forks, overshoes, yoyos, dog bones), then spread the solution on as large an area as you can handle before it dries out. As you're finishing at one end of the room, the solution you first laid down is working actively on the dirt, old wax, spots, stains, and marks. When you return to the first area and begin to mop, wipe, or lightly rub it clean, the area you just left is now under heavy attack by the liquid, and most of the cleaning will have been accomplished by the time you get there with the mop.

When we cleaned the big floor in 1¼ hours we spent almost no time scrubbing. We spread the cleaning solution and I ran over the surface with a floor machine (I could also have used a hand floor scrubber—see the Equipment Chart). I didn't try to grind or scrub the floor clean—I covered it quickly to loosen the surface dirt so the chemical solution could do the work. By the time I reached the far end of the room, the solution spread on the first part had dissolved and suspended the dirty old wax. The next pass over the same area caused every drop of dirt and wax to come off. We immediately squeegeed the floor and picked up the gunk with a plain old dustpan and put it in a bucket. (This eliminated the need for a "slop mop.") The floor squeegeed (see Equipment Chart) clean, then only needed to be mopped with clear water. One mop bucket did the whole floor!

In cases where all the dirt and wax won't quite come off and scrubbing seems called for, it's generally your own fault—by failing to perform good regular cleaning, you've allowed a thick layer of wax and dirt to build up. Buildups of various kinds are the greatest obstacle to simple cleaning; they're best exemplified by the old villain hard water. Look at the brand-new sparkling tile in your shower, or your exterior windows. They're going to get hard water on them from use, accident, or irrigation. Residue starts with an innocent thing

called a drop. A drop doesn't seem much of a bother, because if unmolested, it will evaporate away.

At least it will *appear* to leave. A closer examination reveals that each drop has a character called mineral salts, which slide to the bottom of the drop as it evaporates. Though the drop appears to have vanished, a slight deposit of mineral salts remains. Beginning so insignificantly and unseen, it's ignored. Again water is splashed on the surface, new drops form in the place occupied by previous drops, and leave their mineral marks to unite with the existing residue. Six months, sixty showers, or twenty sprinklings later, that innocent first drop has become hard water buildup. If kept clean daily, or in many cases even weekly, it's a two-minute instead of a twenty-minute job. If done annually or "when I get around to it," it's a surface-damaging, chemical-squandering experience that greatly embitters one's attitude toward sanitation.

Scrubbing is never smart!

Give the solution time to work!

Whether cleaning a floor, wall, stovetop, tub, or patio, apply cleaning solution over as large an area as you can handle before it dries. Then let the chemical work. By the time you go back and wipe the area, the surface will for the most part have cleaned itself. If it doesn't come clean, re-apply and wait a bit longer. How much time it takes the solution to deal with the dirt depends on how dirty the surface is. But let the solution do the work! It's a waste of time to concentrate on tiny areas and scrub.

The Basic Principles of Cleaning

Cleaning should be done with your head, not your hands. . . IN FOUR BASIC STEPS:

1. ELIMINATE
Sweep, dustmop, brush, or wipe all dirt, gravel, crumbs, and other loose material from the surface.

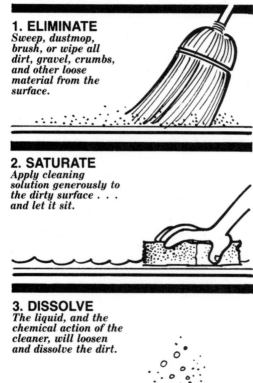

2. SATURATE
Apply cleaning solution generously to the dirty surface . . . and let it sit.

3. DISSOLVE
The liquid, and the chemical action of the cleaner, will loosen and dissolve the dirt.

4. REMOVE
With a sponge, cleaning cloth, or squeegee, remove the now-dissolved mushy dirt.

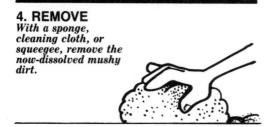

Be sure to touch base

Be sure to match your cleaning agent base to the dirt or soil you're trying to remove. This is a simple but important principle. "Base" in this case simply means dissolving agent. Water won't cut oil because it's the wrong base. Vinegar won't cut grease even for Merlin the Magician. Most household cleaners won't cut oil at all; an inexpensive oil-based solvent or thinner will dissolve it in seconds. When oil or tar gets on walls, floors, rugs, or even clothes, a solvent (like paint thinner, turpentine, or other oil-based cleaner) will break down the tar or oil so that it can be easily wiped away. You can rub and grind contact cement edge slops with every cleaner available and not get anywhere, but if you use a little lacquer thinner or contact cement solvent (again, matching the contact cement base), it's instantly softened and can be wiped off as easily as soft butter out of a dish!

Cleaning preparation labels generally give the base (oil, naphtha, water, etc.). Whenever you're in doubt as to whether a particular base should be used on a particular surface, test it first in an inconspicuous area.

Abrasion evasion

Using powdered cleansers and steel wool to grind dirt off surfaces has become a ritual with too many homemakers. With the same generosity they use to apply powder to the baby's rump, they coat their sinks with cleansing powder and attack them with brisk rubbing. You can actually hear the results as the grinding abrasion quickly removes stains and spots—along with the chrome or porcelain on the unit. The cleanser then has to be flushed off. Some of it will set like concrete in the gooseneck of the sink drain, on the floor, and on the fixtures. The light scum that remains on the sink or tub has to be rubbed and polished off, again wearing away the surface. The damage is gradual but inevitable. On the new fiberglass sinks, tubs, and other fixtures, the damage isn't even that gradual. Fiberglass isn't as tough as the old porcelain and enameled iron. It damages easily and once damaged is a pain to clean.

Even more important, you lose time cleaning by the abrasion method. You should be relaxing to the cleaning principle eliminate—saturate—dissolve—remove. It really works. Discipline yourself to use it, and you'll reward yourself with two hours of free time out of the four hours you once wasted grinding and scrubbing away!

Keep your working stuff near you!

I've heard claims that a homemaker walks eight to fifteen miles a day doing housework. I wouldn't doubt it. I used to walk one mile per room I cleaned until I learned to keep my cleaning tools within reach. Too many people place their tools and buckets in a central "cleaning station" in the room and constantly walk three, four, or even five or six steps back and forth during a project. They spend half of their time and energy traveling.

If you need the exercise, continue to use a central cleaning station. If you want to get the job done and have energy left for a tennis game, bowling, or other personal sporting around, figure out how to keep your tools (sponges, buckets, cloths, screwdriver, etc.) within your reach. (For example, if you're washing cupboards, set your tools on the counter instead of on the floor—same with painting.) If you hang the bucket on the ladder or hold it in your hand, it will save the bend and dip all the way to the floor and back up. Try it—you'll be amazed at the time and effort you save!

Keep spray bottles near the area in which you use them—e.g., keep the disinfectant cleaner in the bathroom. Buy or make yourself a pocketed cleaning apron to keep your dustcloths and cleaning cloths and protective gloves in—and just hang it up when you're through.

The dreaded task: At my housecleaning seminars I always spring the question, "How many of you like to clean windows?" This is always good for a chorus of groans from everyone present. Occasionally, about two out of every thousand will raise an eager hand indicating that they, indeed, do enjoy cleaning windows. (Further investigation reveals why: Both have maids to do the job!) That leaves almost 100 percent of homemakers who hate window cleaning.

The reason is simple. After hours of laboriously polishing windows, you think, "At last. I'm finished!" But hope is dashed when the sun comes up or changes angle. Streaks and smears suddenly appear out of nowhere,

magnified for all to see. You again give the window the old college try—and the smears and streaks only change places. Re-arming yourself with more window cleaner, rags, and gritty determination, you work even harder and faster to get the windows clean, but they seem only to get worse.

Night falls, and so does the curtain, on a crestfallen and discouraged worker. The next morning you go downtown and eye the 50-story solid glass buildings, the huge storefront display windows, and mumble, "That glass is beautiful . . . but I never see anyone cleaning it. How do they keep it so clean?"

The reason we seldom see window cleaners isn't because those windows don't need to be done—most

Don't be caught streaking... windows

commercial windows have to be cleaned more often than house windows. But professional window cleaners only take minutes, not hours, to do their job. Homemakers can be just as effective on their own windows if they learn the basic techniques used by professionals.

The first move toward successful window cleaning is to rid your storage cabinet of all the "glass gleam" garbage you've been trying to make work for years. The main reason your windows streak and seem to get worse is the oily, soapy gunk (including homemade concoctions) you've been smearing on them. Pounds of it have been put on, and only part of it wipes off. Gradually you've built up a layer of transparent waxy material that you spread around

every time you try to clean the window. It not only creates an impossible cleaning situation, it also primes the glass surface to hold dust,

Spraying and rubbing are self-defeating—as you can see as soon as the sun comes up or changes direction.

bug spots, and airborne particles. The result is windows that have to be cleaned more often.

Take heart. It hasn't been your fault all these years. Even the chief window washer for New York City's tallest all-glass buildings couldn't get windows clean without streaks if all he used was the stuff sold to most of the public.

The right way

To recover all those lost polishing hours, let's learn to do windows professionally. Go down to the janitorial supply house and buy a professional-quality brass or stainless steel squeegee (see Equipment Chart).

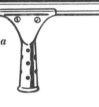

Go to a janitorial supply house and buy a professional-quality squeegee. Make sure the rubber blade laps over both ends, and keep the blade undamaged—don't do anything but clean windows with it.

Ettore Steccone brand is the best! Don't go to the local supermarket or discount house and buy those recycled-truck-tire war clubs they call squeegees. These won't work well even in a professional's hands.

Pick up some window-cleaning solution, which can be either ammonia, or ordinary liquid dish detergent. Both will work well if you use them sparingly; resist the tendency to add too much chemical or detergent to the solution—this causes streaks and leaves residue. One capful is plenty for each gallon of warm water.

Six steps to sparkling windows

1. *Put a capful of ammonia or a couple of drops of dish detergent in a bucket of warm water. There is always a tendency to add too much soap or detergent—this is what causes streaks and leaves residue.*

2. *Wet the window lightly with the solution, using a clean sponge, brush, or wand applicator ("Golden Glove"). You don't need to flood it. You're cleaning it, not baptizing it! If the window is really dirty or has years of "miracle" gunk buildup, go over the moistened area again.*

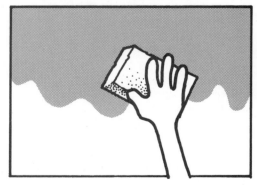

A window can be cleaned from either side or from the top using this technique. Always be sure first to squeegee off that top inch of the glass to eliminate potential dripping. Wipe off the bottom of the window sill with your damp cloth when you're finished.

3. *Wipe the dry rubber blade of your squeegee with a damp cloth or chamois. A dry blade on any dry glass surface will "peep-a-peep" along and skip places.*

4. *Next, tilt the squeegee at an angle to the glass so that only about an inch of the rubber blade presses lightly against the top of the window glass (not the window frame or the house shingles!). Then pull the squeegee across the window horizontally.*

This will leave about a 1-inch dry strip across the top of the window. Remember all those drips that came running down from the top of your clean window when you tried squeegeeing once before? Well, by squeegeeing across the top first, you've removed that potential stream.

5. *Place the squeegee horizontally in the dry area . . .*

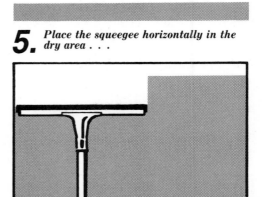

6. *. . . and pull down, lapping over into the dry, clean area each time to prevent any water from running into the cleaned area. Wipe the blade with a damp cloth or chamois after each stroke. Finish with a horizontal stroke across the bottom to remove the water puddled there.*

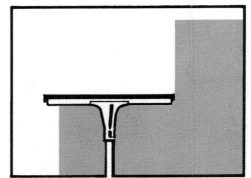

How to get rid
of those last spots

After completing a window, you undoubtedly will detect a tiny drop or squeegee mark or two and a little moisture on the edges of the glass near the frame. Your old tendency was to snatch a dry cloth and with a fingertip under it wipe off the edge. I can assure you this will leave a finger-wide mark right down that edge. Once you notice that, the temptation will be to wipe it again, this time with a bundled cloth. Then you'll have a 4-inch mark and have to re-clean the whole window.

After squeegeeing the window, just leave those little beads of side moisture. They'll disappear and you'll

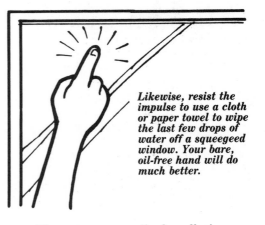

Likewise, resist the impulse to use a cloth or paper towel to wipe the last few drops of water off a squeegeed window. Your bare, oil-free hand will do much better.

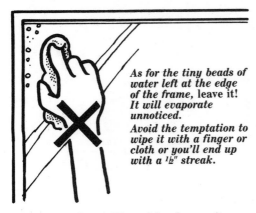

As for the tiny beads of water left at the edge of the frame, leave it! It will evaporate unnoticed.

Avoid the temptation to wipe it with a finger or cloth or you'll end up with a ½" streak.

never see them. Your friends won't, either, unless they bring their opera glasses with them.

As for middle-of-the-window drops or tiny squeegee lines, do not use a cloth (Law: There is no such thing as a lint-free or mark-free cloth in window cleaning). Because you've been working in the solution, your bare hand will be oil-free and you can use a dry finger to wipe marks away without leaving a blemish.

The squeegee method really is as easy as it sounds. It's three to five times faster than the old way. It will use only a penny or two worth of cleaner and leave your windows pure and clean to repel particles and dirt. Remember, glass is more susceptible to airborne dirt than any other material in the house: Windows are a prime surface for grime from cooking, chemical film from air pollution, bug specks, etc. Try to keep your windows so clean and slick that flies lose their footing. Squeaky-clean glass will repel marks—even fingerprints—much better than glass with a coat of wax or soap scum on it.

It's worth the effort to work on your squeegee technique for a while, since it will be awkward at first. All of that accumulated gunk might take a little extra effort to remove. Once you catch on, you'll love it and wish you had more windows to do.

Learning to clean windows fast and effectively will change your outlook on life. You'll cherish the cute little handprints, enjoy watching frustrated insects slip off the glass, and even tolerate the sweet birdies who occasionally befoul your windows.

Problem areas

Squeegees will work on any normal household window (but not on textured or stained glass, for instance), and they come in sizes to fit the task at hand. Squeegees can also be cut with a hacksaw to custom-fit small panes if you so desire. Pull the rubber blade out of the channel before cutting, and then cut the rubber about ¼ inch longer than the remodeled blade (so it will extend ⅛ inch at each end).

My advice regarding tiny little windows is to let them go as long as possible, because the optical illusion created by the small surfaces hides marks, specks, and smudges. When they do need cleaning, depending on their size, either a squeegee or a trigger-spray bottle filled with evaporating (alcohol-based) window cleaner can be used.

If you're not too particular, I'd just brush off the outside, hose them down, rinse them, and call it good. I don't think any window in a home is worth numerous hours of work. Big windows show dirt and streaks more readily than small panes, which look more "romantic" a bit hazy.

There are times and places in small, confined areas where a spray bottle with an evaporating cleaning solution is more efficient to use (handprints on glass entrance doors, mirrors, decorative doors and windows, etc.). You can obtain an inexpensive window-cleaning solution of this type in concentrated form from a janitorial supply house, dilute it with water, spray it lightly on soiled glass, then buff it dry with a cotton cloth or a "hard" (read cheap) paper towel (the soft expensive ones leave lint like crazy). *Don't* use newspaper. The quick-drying solution won't leave a waxy buildup and allows you to "polish" the glass. Only slight sheens and streaks are left, which are seldom noticeable in such small areas.

When windows are out of reach for easy hand or ladder squeegee work, a pole or extension handle of any length you can maneuver will work on the same principle surprisingly well. Clean glass always looks good. A few tiny smudges or drips won't hurt anything, so don't try to be a perfectionist. It

Washing high windows

Clean glass always looks good. When windows are out of reach for easy hand or ladder work, a squeegee handle of any length you can maneuver will work on the same principle with surprising accuracy. I use a 4 to 8-foot Steccone extension handle. A few tiny smudges or drips won't hurt anything, so don't try to be a perfectionist. It isn't worth the stress or time.

◀**EXTENSION HANDLE**

Second story windows can be done easily and your feet never leave the ground. No ladder is needed and there's no safety risk.

isn't worth the stress or time. I use a 4- to 8-foot Ettore Steccone extension handle. Even second-story windows are quick to do and your feet never leave the ground. You don't need a ladder and there's no safety risk.

If you have hard water buildup from irrigation or sprinkling your lawn, don't use abrasive cleanser or the glass will cloud and scratch. There are some mild professional and consumer phosphoric acid cleaners that will remove the deposit. Once you've done that, keep hard water off with regular maintenance or an adjustment in your sprinkling system.

When window casings and trim get older, paint and putty chips catch under the squeegee blade and make cleaning miserable. New aluminum or well-maintained wood won't give you any grief. Taking the time to sand and repaint or reglaze will save you many cleaning hours.

If your squeegee blade gets damaged and starts leaving a line of solution on your windows, pull it out of the channel, turn it over, and snap it back in. When the blade finally wears out or rounds out, just buy a new blade and snap it into the squeegee channel. (Be sure 1/8 inch of the blade extends beyond each end of the channel.)

Most window damage (aside from breaking them) occurs when labels are being removed from new windows or paint or mortar from new or old ones. There are four rules in performing cleanup operations on glass:

1. *Always keep the glass surface wet. The foreign material you're trying to remove will then generally slide or float off.*

2. *Use only razor-sharp blades or flat razor-type tools in a one-way forward motion, then lift the tool off*

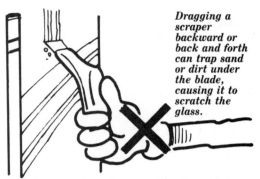

Dragging a scraper backward or back and forth can trap sand or dirt under the blade, causing it to scratch the glass.

the glass and make another forward stroke. Never go back and forth. Pulling the tool back and forth will eventually trap a piece of grit or sand behind and under the blade, which will scratch even a wet window (you'll never rub that one off with a de-oiled bare hand, either).

3. *Don't use abrasive scrub pads or compounds on window glass.*

4. *Be careful. Too much pressure, or an abrupt or careless motion, could get you a nasty cut as well as a broken pane.*

In general, windows are high-maintenance areas, and there's a lot more than glass to keep clean and dust-free. Fortunately, just as professional window-washing methods can have glass looking its best with minimum effort on your part, a little attention to technique can keep your screens, blinds, and curtains looking sharp.

How to clean . . .

Drapes

Buy good-quality drapes, and check regularly to make sure they stay hung properly. Vacuum drape tops and sides occasionally. When you're cleaning the floor near full-length drapes you can protect them by slipping the bottom of the panel through an ordinary clothes hanger and hooking the top over the rod.

You can refurbish drapes not dirty enough to be cleaned by running them through the clothes dryer on a cool setting. (*Don't* do this with fiberglass drapes; they'll leave an irritating residue in the dryer that will transfer itself to clothing.) Be sure to remove the drapery hooks first.

Since drapes are relatively inexpensive to dry clean, get estimates from different shops. It's often less of a hassle than doing them yourself.

Screens

When your screens become embedded with dead bugs, tree sap, dirt, bird droppings, seeds, and other unsightly debris, take them down. Carry them outside, spread out a big cloth, old rug, or piece of canvas, and *lay them flat* (this is important to avoid damage) on it. Mix up a light neutral cleaner solution and scrub them with a soft-bristled brush. Rinse the screens with a hose, give them a sharp rap with your hand to jar most of the water loose, and let them finish drying in the sun.

Blinds

Whether the old Venetian type or the new minis, blinds are such a pain to dust and wash that some homemakers have cheerfully given up the privacy and easy daylight-adjustment benefits blinds undeniably provide. If you haven't yet reached that point, you might never have to if you clean blinds this way. Keep blinds dusted with a Masslinn cloth (see Equipment Chart) to keep them looking good as long as possible. Eventually, though, they'll need to be washed. Don't try to do this without taking them down; washing blinds in place is slow and messy and you'll curse yourself for attempting it. Don't try washing them in the sink or bathtub, either. Take them outside. Find a slanting surface if you can; if not, flat will do. But you *must* lay an old quilt, blanket, cloth, or piece of canvas under the blinds to prevent damage.

Let each blind out to full length. Make sure the louvers are flat. Lay the blind down on the cloth and scrub in the direction of the slats, using a soft-bristled brush and a neutral cleaner solution. Then reverse the blind and wash the other side. The cushioning cloth will get soapy and help clean the blind.

Hang or hold the blind up and rinse it with a hose (a helper is very useful at this point). Shake the excess water off and let the blind dry thoroughly before re-hanging it.

8.

*What do we do with
the dirt on the farm?*

*It flies from the road
and comes straight
from the barn.*

*It pours through the
windows and tracks
on the floors.*

*We give up and just
plant our garden
indoors.*

—Marilyn May

Prevention — keeping the enemy out

Mats: a must

A new hospital, nestled in a valley with one of the world's most famous ski resorts, had been in operation for two years when its housekeeping personnel retired. Replacements were needed and a professional cleaning service was contracted. Following careful measurement of the space, occupancy, conditions, and after interviews with the retiring staff members, it was concluded that a total of twelve hours of work was required each night to clean the offices, public area, entrances, and medical administrative wing. When signing the contract, the owner of the janitorial company made one explicit request. Both entrances to the hospital were to be covered with vinyl-backed nylon mat running at least fifteen feet inside both entrances. There had been no mats before because it was thought they might detract from the hospital's alpine beauty. The hospital's administrator agreed to order the doormats that day.

The cleaning company began their service and were spending twelve hours plus a few extra daily to keep the place up to standard. They wet-mopped nightly, used six treated dust-control cloths on the floor, and had to scrub some areas every week with their floor machines. Anticipating the difference the new mats would make, the cleaning company owner had the sweeping and vacuuming crew keep track of residue collected from the floors throughout the building. Each night a gallon can was half-filled with gravel, sand, thread, pine needles, and every other thing common to a resort area. Three weeks later, the mats arrived and were installed at both entrances.

The first night the mats were in place, the hours of work dropped to ten, and the sweeping residue was reduced to half a quart of gum wrappers, toothpicks, etc. After one week, the new mats reduced the cleaning to nine hours per night. The dustcloths were reduced from six to two, wet-mopping was reduced to twice a week, and dusting to every other night. Cleaning supplies were cut more than 50 percent. The mats cost $240 and were paid for in less than one week in labor and cleaning supplies saved. A decrease in slips and entrance falls was noted, and the mats lasted for four years!

Mats protect your house.

Proper matting alone can save the average household approximately 200 hours of work a year, slow down structure depreciation, and save over $100 in direct cleaning supply costs. The cost of matting for the average home is about $80-$120. But it's the 200 hours that's the big savings for you. That's thirty minutes a day cut from your chore time with no effort expended.

The reasons for such savings of time, effort, money, and depreciation are easy to understand if you simply ask yourself, "What is it that I clean out of my house, off my rugs, off the walls, off the furniture, the pictures, etc.?" Dust and dirt are the obvious answers. Where does it come from? Almost 100 percent of it comes from the outside. How does it get inside? Eighty percent of it is *transported* in (the rest leaks through cracks, is airborne, or originates inside). The average five-person home accumulates forty pounds of dust—composed of everything from air pollution particles and topsoil to dead insects and pet dander—a year. Most dirt or residue is carried into the home via the clothes and the feet.

Professionals estimate that it costs $600 a pound to remove dirt once it's inside. It costs *you* even more in time:

1. *You shampoo carpets because of that dirt embedded in them.*

2. *You strip and wax the floor because of that dirt embedded in it.*

3. *You dust, dust, dust because of that dirt circulating in the air.*

4. *You wash clothes more often because of that dirt.*

5. *Your cleaning equipment and supplies wear out faster because of that dirt.*

Proper matting will:

1. *Keep your house cleaner.*

2. *Reduce the need for shampooing, waxing, and washing.*

3. *Absorb sound.*

4. *Enhance safety.*

5. *Improve appearance.*

All this saves you both time and money. It takes one piece of equipment and a few minutes to get dirt out of a mat. It takes ten pieces of equipment and hours to get it out of your home!

Where is your carpet the dirtiest? At the entrance, on about a 3x4-foot square where the matting should be. It's only logical—if dirt doesn't get in, you won't have to round it up. As a person criticizing mats once said, "Bah! I hate doormats—all they are is dirt catchers!" I rest my case.

Taking advantage of good matting is the smartest, easiest, and least expensive thing you can do to cut your housecleaning time. It's easier to vacuum or shake out a mat daily than it is to chase dirt all over the house. Look at the hospital. The distributed dirt and debris were reduced from one-half gallon to one pint. Mats will perform a great service in your home. Don't take my word for it—try it! You'll cry over the lost years of labor and money you've wasted by not getting adequate mats sooner. Instead of scrubbing your floor weekly, you could end up doing it annually. (I've even had one commercial building go *five years* and the floor finish still looked good.)

If you have good matting, all the fine gravel, grit, and dirt that hangs on the bottoms of shoes and scratches, soils, and discolors will be out of action. Waxed floors last a long time when they aren't abused by grit. Next time you go into an office building, notice the difference in the floor on the lower level as compared to the upper-level floors. Even if the traffic is the same, the upper ones will last twice as long and look twice as good because the grit doesn't get to them. Traffic doesn't hurt a floor much—it's the abrasiveness of dirt that creates havoc. Keep it out of your home, and you'll keep yourself out of the crouching, scrubbing position. Now, that's the

sensible way to clean house—not to have to do it in the first place!

Here are some matting pointers that will advance your goal of gaining thirty "free" minutes a day.

Some mats to sidestep

Avoid decorative mats. We all love to see our name in print—even on a worthless rubber doormat. Get rid of

Avoid using leftover carpet squares.

Don't use clothbacks.

Get rid of link or perforated mats.

How to mat an entrance

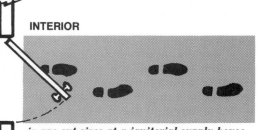

EXTERIOR   **DOOR**   **INTERIOR**

Use commercial, nylon-tuft mats inside and synthetic-grass or rough textured mats outside. These mats are available in a wide range of colors and can be obtained in rolls or in pre-cut sizes at a janitorial supply house. For best results, the mats should be long enough to allow four steps on each.

it! It isn't doing much good, and the time it takes to clean around it is probably greater than the cleaning time it saves. Link mats (the kind made from little slices of old car tires wired together) are ineffective for most homes and extremely dangerous for wearers of high heels. Coco mats are more trouble than they're worth because they don't absorb well and they shed. Have you ever tried to clean a coco mat? That alone should convince you not to buy one!

For outside the house, the synthetic-grass-type mats or any rough-textured nonperforated mat with a rubber back is good. These won't rot, they're easy to clean, and they'll knock the big stuff off the shoes or boots of the person coming into your home. Try to get a 5-foot or longer mat to cover three or four steps. The exact type of exterior mat to buy depends on the space available, overhead cover (awning or porch), if any, your home and landscaping style, and how bad thievery is in the neighborhood.

On the inside

The first thing to do is get rid of any carpet samples or scraps you're using for "throw rugs." These items are, indeed, appropriately named. The jute backing and curling edges throw their users into the hospital. They're unsafe, unattractive, and more to the point, inefficient. Get rid of them!

At any janitorial supply house, you can buy commercial grade, vinyl- or rubber-backed nylon mats. This type of mat for inside areas of the home helps to reduce falls and trap loose dirt—the same dirt you'd be cleaning from everything in the house. They are efficient, will last up to fifteen years, and are available in a wide variety of colors. They come in widths of three, four, or six feet, and in any length. The nylon creates a static charge that actually helps pull particles from your shoes and clothes. They will absorb mud and water from foot traffic and

It takes one piece of equipment and a few minutes to get dirt out of a mat. It takes ten pieces of equipment and hours to get it out of your home!

hold it in the roots of the mat. They won't show dirt easily and can be vacuumed like any other carpet.

Some mats will creep a little on some surfaces, and a "rug hugger" type with a textured back can be purchased if you get tired of retrieving the carpet.

An often forgotten area in our homes that should also be well matted is the garage entrance. Plenty of sawdust, oil stains, and project residue get tracked into the house from the garage. Fine silt, sand, and gravel piled up on the road often get caught up in the snow that lodges under a car and falls loose on the garage floor. When it melts, the sand and grit are carried into the house by foot. Concrete dust and garage-type soils and dirt are abrasive to carpet and waxed floors.

Apartments, condominiums, and motor homes need to be matted, too. The slightly smaller amount of dirt and debris that might get to the eighth floor of a modern apartment building is multiplied by the fact that it's gritty city dirt that has a smaller area over which to distribute itself—hence the soiling and damage to the dwelling can be as acute as in a large, dust-surrounded farmhouse.

A 3x5-foot mat is an excellent all-purpose size. It's wide enough to cover an average doorway, long enough to cover four entrance steps, and light enough to handle and to clean. An extra 3x12-foot runner can be rolled up and kept for remodeling, parties, or wet weather. This extra mat will be a good investment if your traffic, lifestyle, and location merit it. It would be an especially good idea for a new home, since it's common for a family to move in before the landscaping is

completed. The several months of working on the yard generates a lot of mud, and the resulting damage is often unnoticed because the house is new.

Not only will you save thirty minutes a day when you install adequate matting, but your doorways and entrances will be better looking, quieter, and safer. Get mats before you start to clean, and you won't have to start as soon or work as long.

To maintain mats:

Keep them vacuumed.

When they're dirty, hose them down, apply neutral cleaner solution, scrub a bit, and hose them again.

Squeegee off excess water with a floor squeegee or old window squeegee.

Hang mats to dry. Never use them when the back is wet.

Other preventive measures

Now that you have your mats lying in wait for all that creeping dirt, you ought to set up a few more culprit catchers for the things that cause housework. Remember again, the idea isn't to get faster or bigger, better tools to beat the dirtiers: The first principle of cleaning is not to have to do it in the first place. . . .

Cure litter

Make it a hard and fast rule in your home that everyone picks up his or her own litter and is responsible for personal belongings. And make it relatively simple for everyone to abide by the rule. Provide waste containers for *every* room in the house, and outside where the kids play. Empty the containers frequently before the contents become attractive to germs, insects, and larger animals.

Make sure there are shelves, drawers, racks, hooks, and toy boxes enough for everyone to put away his or her belongings quickly and easily. If there's a place to put it, chances are 60 percent better that it'll end up where it ought to (rather than on the couch, the bed, the floor, the stairs).

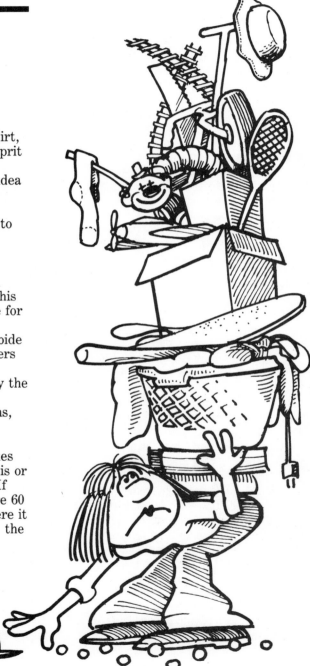

The trouble with cleaning up litter is that when you're finished you're right where you should have been before you started!

Animals

There's no getting around the fact that house animals create housework and cause damage, but you can minimize it. My choice, depending on the animal and where you live, is to keep it outside, but that's not always possible. If you do have an indoor/outdoor pet, consider installing a pet door so it can come in and go out at will. This saves wear and tear on the people door if your pet's a scratch-at-the-door type (and it saves you from being the animal's door person).

Both cats and dogs should be brushed regularly and their claws trimmed. Your vet can show you how to do this. Dogs should be bathed as soon as they start smelling "doggy." A pet rake—cheap to buy and worth every penny—will be a big help in coping with shedding hair.

Vacuum pet hair off upholstered furniture. Better yet, keep animals off furniture, or designate one chair that's theirs, and keep a throw cover over it that you can wash easily.

Build your cat a good scratching post. Make sure it's tall enough for the cat to stretch full length (a section of de-barked log is good), and weight the base so the cat can't tip it over. If you cover it with carpeting, use the loopy kind that will engage the cat's claws. Don't use shag; the cat won't.

Use a disinfectant cleaner when you clean up after animals.

Mildew

Mildew looks bad and can be damaging, but it isn't really a cleaning problem. Mildew is a spore fungus that thrives on moisture and temperatures between 75° and 85°F. There are five ways to prevent or retard mildew growth:

1. *Never put anything away wet (laundry, camping gear, etc.).*
2. *Well-lighted areas don't agree with mildew. Light prevents its growth and can even kill it.*
3. *Proper ventilation helps prevent mildew spore growth.*
4. *Cleaning all mildew-prone areas with a diluted disinfectant solution will slow down or stop growth.*
5. *Packets of silica gel in small, enclosed, chronically mildewed places (drawers, shoes) absorb moisture and can minimize mildew growth.*

Cigarette mess

One of the most effective preventive measures you can take is to eliminate smoking from your home. In commercial buildings almost 30 percent of cleaning costs stem from smoking residue, waste, and damage.

All of us pay a small fortune for the smoking habit—it costs taxpayers millions of dollars daily.

Smoking also causes a high percentage of fatal and damaging fires, and can make many jobs unsafe.

Smoke dirties the windows, yellows the light fixtures above, cuts the efficiency of energy expenditure, soils and ruins the acoustical tile of the ceiling, smells up the upholstery, and burns and damages the carpet and floor. Eyes water, lungs fill with smoke, clothes and hair are saturated offensively. Who would consider taking out a miniature incinerator and burning paper, leaves, and trash whenever they got the urge? But that's what a smoker does.

In trying to correct the problem, we designate special smoking areas, make better filters, bigger ashtrays, better vents and room deodorizers, better gargles and tooth polishes, develop lung transplants, etc., but this is like building a bigger drawer, closet, or garage when the others get full: The problem is still there, doing damage, only contained.

The simplest, cheapest, most effective approach is to de-junk the habit; then the problem will be cut off at the source.

When you're away

If you leave home for a while, your home can help clean itself if you let it. Shut off all dripping faucets. In winter, turn off the water at the main valve and empty all the pipes, or leave the heat high enough that a sudden cold snap won't freeze and burst the pipes. Make sure all the toilets are flushed;

stretching a piece of plastic wrap over toilet bowls will minimize evaporation and prevent a mineral deposit ring. Don't leave any fruit or food out to attract insects or rodents, and be sure to take the garbage out. If possible, don't leave any dirty laundry in the hamper or elsewhere. Unplug all appliances except for the refrigerator, freezer, dehumidifier, and other house-maintaining systems. Close the drapes (where you can without a security risk) to prevent sun fading of carpets and upholstery. Be sure to close all interior doors so that if a fire should start, it might choke itself out. You'll feel better about leaving, and great about coming home.

Keep up

Finally, remember: Dirty by the inch is a cinch; by the yard, it's hard.

Don't get buried alive—clean as you go. Who wants to finish an overhaul, a paint job, or any project and have to clean the entire mess at the end? Clean and put everything back as soon as you're finished using it. If you let it all pile up for a big cleaning spree, it's emotional and physical suicide.

And DON'T CLEAN THINGS THAT AREN'T DIRTY. You can go months without doing windows and vacuuming in certain places. Too many people think they have a moral obligation to do it "every day" or "once a week" or "once a month." You clean to prevent unhealthiness, ugliness, and depreciation. If a little dirt or dust causes none of these, darned if I'm going to flounder around with a broom and a bucket.

It's tough and time-consuming to clean a cluttered roomscape. Keep your home picked up; put everything away as soon as you use it.

Check ✓ before you clean it

Fix those items that always slow you up and cause you to do everything more than once (or actually *add* to your cleaning chores!)

Some things aren't worth doing. Some *can't* be cleaned. Others will look tacky even when they're clean and orderly. Taking care of these items first will not only make cleaning and maintenance easier, but will make you feel better (which makes everything easier). Eliminate or remove anything that bugs you—that's inconvenient, no longer functional, or that you just don't like. REMEMBER—the first principle of efficient cleaning is to not have to do it in the first place. Check these things before you start.

☐ **Be sure you have plenty of convenient, roomy litter receptacles. You'll do less cleaning and picking up.**

☐ **Be sure you have enough towel racks.**

☐ **Be sure all closets have an adequate supply of hangers.**

☐ **Eliminate furniture you don't use or need. It has no value and magnifies your cleaning chores.**

☐ **Eliminate excess playthings (children and adults). Unused tennis rackets, snowmobiles, motorbikes, TV games that have fallen from favor, old hobby supplies, puzzles with "only one piece missing."**

☐ **Get anything that can be wall-mounted off the floor. It'll make cleaning a lot easier and curb accumulation. (And eye-level things are easier to see and safer to use.)**

☐ **See that your cooking exhaust is vented.**

☐ **Make sure all dirt and air leakage into the house is stopped. Cracks in the foundation, too, let dust and moisture into the house, causing damage and additional cleaning time.**

- [ ] Make sure your vacuum works perfectly.

- [ ] Seal all concrete floor surfaces for easy maintenance.

- [ ] Paint or seal (varnish) all surfaces that can't be easily dusted, washed, or cleaned.

- [ ] Repair/replace all damaged surfaces. Paint, patch, or panel so they can be easily maintained.

- [ ] Alter any physical surface or appearance you don't like. Paint it, sand it, cover it, or give it away.

- [ ] See that drawer hardware is tight and that drawers slide easily.

- [ ] Make sure that all doors close tightly and easily. A light sanding and two coats of polyurethane or varnish will make wooden doors bright and easily cleanable, and doortops smooth and easily dustable.

- [ ] Be sure that all windows slide open and shut (and lock) easily—and cracks are sealed.

- [ ] Repair every leaky or dripping fixture.

- [ ] Fix or tighten all clotheslines, stair railings, etc. Check all the hardware around the house. Remember,
    > A 50¢ screw or bolt
    > can save a $5 hinge . . .
    > A $50 door . . .
    > A $500 robbery . . .
    > A $5,000 fire!

- [ ] See that light bulbs that need replacing are replaced, and light fixtures are tightened.

- [ ] Get rid of all shin and head bumpers (countertops, ledges, and furniture that bash you every time you pass by, or straighten up).

- [ ] Adjust every shelf to the height you really want and need.

9.

Floors under your foot & rule

The floor, more than any other part of the house, projects the overall image of your home. The chances of anyone's noticing that all-day sucker stuck to the patio door, the half-eaten wiener on the bookcase, or the cobweb across Grandpa's picture are lessened if the floors are clean and brilliant. Fortunately, maintaining beautiful floors is one of the simplest jobs in the house. (Trust me.)

The term "hard floors" didn't originate as a description of the effort needed to clean them; it's simply used to distinguish them from soft floors (carpets). Hard floors include linoleum, wood, ceramic and other tiles, terrazzo, cork, dirt (nothing under it), and good old concrete. All hard floors have their purpose, and they all have to be cleaned and maintained.

Proper floor care can be a lifesaver for you physically and emotionally. There are four reasons for you to learn and apply good floor care practices:

1. Appearance
A beautiful floor is an exhilarating experience for the beholder and a reward for the homemaker.

2. Protection
Even the hardest surfaces will scuff, wear, and dull with grinding foot traffic, spills, and chemical cleaners. A wax or other protective finish covering the surface lessens abrasion and other damage and lengthens the life of the floor. Even the new "no-wax" floors *do* need a dressing or finish to prevent an eventually dull and damaged surface.

3. Cleanability
Soil, dirt, spills, marks of all kinds, and abrasive residues are much simpler to clean from a smooth, well-waxed or finished surface. Sweeping a well-used unwaxed or unfinished tile floor will take you 25 percent longer than sweeping a highly polished one. A coat of wax or other finish on the floor is like a coat of varnish on a bare wood picnic table: It keeps soils and oils from penetrating the surface. Wiping something from the top of a protective nonpenetrable finish takes only seconds. It sure beats spending hours trying to scrub it out once it has soaked in and stained.

4. Safety
Contrary to what most people think, shiny, well-waxed and properly maintained floors are generally much less slippery than bare floors. Bare, porous, worn floors have a slick, flint-hard surface whether wet or dry.

A waxed floor is safer

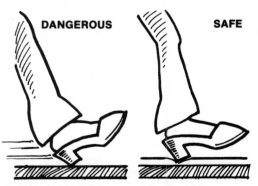

Clean, waxed floors are safer than bare, untreated floors. Wax "cushions" the surface and actually helps prevent slipping.

A coat or two of wax or acrylic finish actually cushions the floor. This could be compared to laying a thin cloth or cover over a bare plastic tabletop: It creates a surface that won't let things slide around. Thus a coat or "cover" of wax makes most floors less slippery.

Just another reminder: Floors require less cleaning if you provide adequate entrance matting (see Chapter 8). Hundreds of hours of floor problems and worries will disappear if you install adequate matting at entrances to stop dirt and abrasives from getting into your house. Some discoloration and wear of waxes comes with time and exposure to sunlight. But most discoloration of wax or finish and deterioration of flooring material comes from dirt penetrating into the wax and eventually to the floor surface. Keeping the surface clean will greatly prolong the life of the finish.

I'm often asked whether hard or soft floors are easier to keep clean. The answer is, it depends. In high traffic or high abuse areas, hard flooring is better. In low traffic, low abuse areas, carpeting is easier and faster to take care of than a hard surface.

How to clean hard floors

The equipment needed to clean your floors depends on the amount and type of hard-surfaced floors you have. During the last twenty years, wall-to-wall carpet has found its way into more and more of the new houses built, often leaving only kitchen and bathroom with hard floors. If a hard floor is in the center of the house where considerable travel over carpeted areas is required to reach it, that hard-floor finish will last for months, if it's kept clean. You could do it by hand in about fifteen minutes a year. A standard sponge mop—the kind with the built-in squeeze lever—is adequate damp-mopping equipment in 80 percent of modern homes.

If you have several rooms of vinyl, linoleum, quarry tile, wood floors as well as a big game room, garage, converted patio, or storage area, some basic labor-saving floor tools would be a good investment. The chart in Chapter 5 outlines what I'd suggest. Get a good 16-ounce wet mop, preferably rayon layflat, and a good mop bucket with a built-in roller-type wringer (Geerpress #180 is a nice heavy-duty one if you have a great deal of hard flooring; a Roller Queen is a good lighter model for less hard floor

Damp mop

Don't make it difficult. Generally, a sponge mop will do fine. Always go over the area twice while it's damp.

First time—wets it. Second time—picks up dirt. Keep your mop clean! Always squeeze the dirty water into the slop bucket before you dip the mop back into the cleaning solution.

area). Wringing mops by hand is finger suicide: The pins, glass, etc., your mop picks up will lacerate your hands. The price of a small commercial mop bucket might shock you, but gasp once or twice and buy it anyway. It will be a time-saver and greatly contribute to the quality of work you can do.

Keep it clean

Again, the most important factor in saving time and keeping maintenance of your floor to a minimum is simple: Keep it clean! That doesn't just mean removing roller skates, cat toys, coins, combs, and clothes, either. It's the dust, grit, gravel, sand, food crumbs, and other such substances that remain on floors, abrade them, and eventually get ground into powder and embed themselves in the surface that cause your cleaning woes. Once all this "dirt power" is on the loose, it will destroy a floor rapidly. Keep hard floors well swept (even when you can't see dirt and dust). Where possible, use a commercial 12- or 18-inch treated dust mop. It's faster, more effective, and will last much longer than anything you can pick up at the supermarket.

Wax it!

As I said earlier, most hard floors need a protective coating. Floors will wear out much faster if they're not protected. Floors claiming to be "no-wax" will also dull in traffic areas if not protected by a finish of some kind. The "never need to wax" claim just doesn't hold up. If you expect such a floor to stay shiny in heavy traffic areas, it needs a dressing.

First, take the old wax off

Once the hard floor is prepared by sweeping and you know the old wax or finish is due to come off, it's time to make that hard job an easy one. Arrive at the scene with two buckets: an ordinary bucket and a mop bucket. Fill the mop bucket three-quarters full of clean water; don't put cleaner in it. Mix some warm water and wax stripper in the ordinary bucket. A detergent cleaner will do fine for a light scrub, but if you want all the wax off, use a commercial wax remover. Ammonia cuts wax, but it can also cut the plasticizers in the floor if you leave it on too long! A non-ammoniated commercial wax remover will do the best and safest job.

Dip your fresh mop into the solution and apply to the floor generously so that the solution can attack the old wax or dirt. Cover as large an area as you feel you can clean and take up before it dries. (About 10x10-foot—you'll learn how much to do if it dries on you once.) Remember, you're using the basic principle of cleaning explained in Chapter 6. As soon as the solution is on the floor old wax and dirt begin to be dissolved and suspended, and can soon be wiped off easily.

This may be a bit optimistic, because chances are you have some spots where wax is built up thick as cardboard and hard as a bullet. It will need scrubbing or scraping, and possibly another application or two of solution. If so, scrub (and not on your hands and knees, either). If you don't have a floor machine, get a hand floor scrubber like the Scrubbee-doo. A Scrubbee-doo has a long handle with a plastic "gripper" on its end that holds a flat 5x10-inch nylon pad. Edges, especially, are easy with one of these little gems. I think one hand floor scrubber could outdo five of those small electric twin-brush scrubbers. (If you do use a floor machine, use nylon scrubbing pads on it. Brushes are almost worthless. For wax removal, the brown or black Pros are the best.)

When the solution on the floor looks gunky and creamy, it means the dirt and old wax are coming loose. Before you clean the stripper and gunk off, check the scrubbed floor with your fingernail. If, after a scrape across the floor, your nail looks like your son's, wax is still there. Use more solution

The right way to remove old wax

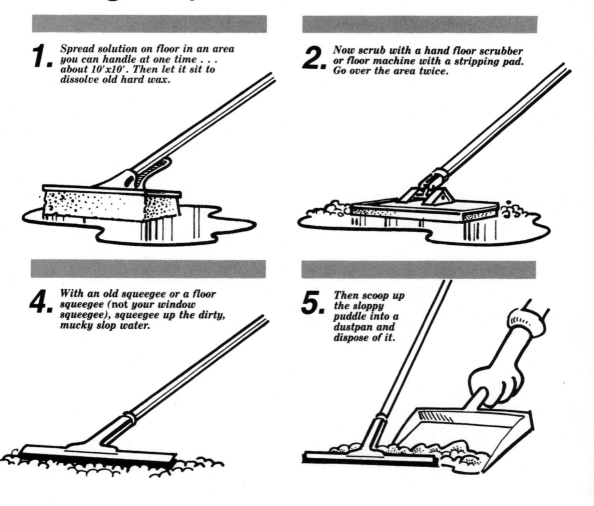

1. Spread solution on floor in an area you can handle at one time . . . about 10'x10'. Then let it sit to dissolve old hard wax.

2. Now scrub with a hand floor scrubber or floor machine with a stripping pad. Go over the area twice.

4. With an old squeegee or a floor squeegee (not your window squeegee), squeegee up the dirty, mucky slop water.

5. Then scoop up the sloppy puddle into a dustpan and dispose of it.

and if necessary scrub a little. If you're on the verge of passing out from exhaustion, you're in an ideal frame of mind to resolve not to let your floor ever get in this condition again and to save yourself hundreds of future scrubbing hours.

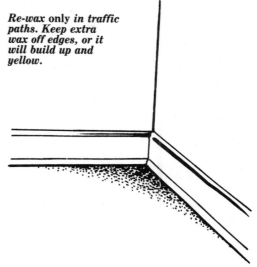

Re-wax only in traffic paths. Keep extra wax off edges, or it will build up and yellow.

3. *Test the floor with a fingernail to see if all the old wax is dissolved.*

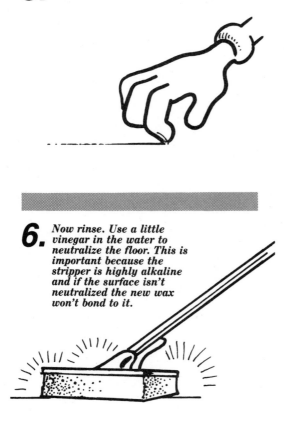

6. *Now rinse. Use a little vinegar in the water to neutralize the floor. This is important because the stripper is highly alkaline and if the surface isn't neutralized the new wax won't bond to it.*

Most floor-cleaning time is spent trying to get wax off unused areas, such as under the lamp table and TV, and off the edges of the floors. Previously, when you rewaxed the traffic paths or worn areas that needed it, you also gave the edges, the areas beneath furniture, and all the other places that didn't need it a generous coat. This system of application was repeated year after year. A traffic pattern area will come clean easily because there's no buildup, but the thick areas will need lots of work to get the buildup off. Next time, don't re-wax the floors where you don't use them. Once you've given the entire floor one coat of wax and more coats are to be applied, put the additional coats *on traffic areas only.*

Now, back to cleaning the floor. The floor is soaked and scrubbed, the wax and dirt are loosened, and it's a mess. Don't pull out that mop and try to sop or slop it up. Instead, reach for a simple, inexpensive tool called a floor squeegee. Get the 15- or 18-inch push-pull type (Ettore Steccone), not the heavy garage type, or, better yet, use an old window squeegee you have lying around (not your nice new one, which should be used only for windows). Squeegee the gunk into a puddle on the uncleaned area (mind you don't squeegee it down a heating vent), and use an ordinary dustpan and empty bucket to quickly scoop the gunk up. (I once met a woman who uses her turkey baster to suck it up, but I'm sticking with the dustpan.) The squeegeed area (except for a possible drop or two from the squeegee lap) will be almost perfectly clean. A squeegee will do about the best possible job on floor coverings that have those little indentations—design impressions of various kinds. (Such floors are the "pits" to clean, for the most part. If you have a wet-dry vacuum [see Equipment Chart], use it instead!)

Now for the mop. Rinse it in clear water and then damp-mop the area. Add a little vinegar to the mop water to neutralize any alkaline residue from the cleaner so the wax will apply better. If the floor was really gunky, rinse again with clean water. Let the floor dry, and that area is ready to wax. Repeat this process until the whole floor is finished. All the gunk will end up in one bucket to be dumped in the toilet (*not* the sink). The mop water will remain fresh and work for the entire floor because it only rinses the squeegeed floor. (And just think—you never had your hands in filthy water.)

When the floor is dry, apply a first light coat of wax to the entire floor. Put two more thin coats on your traffic paths; don't re-wax areas that don't get heavy wear. I'd use a good commercial metal interlock or polymer finish, obtainable at any janitorial supply house.

Tile floors

There must be 400 exotic breeds of stone, brick, ceramic, quarry, and other tile flooring. Like all other floors, they need to be maintained; don't believe any "never need to wax" sales pitch you might be given. The exception is glazed ceramic tile, which needs no finish (but the grout should be sealed).

Any varnish-type finish you put on tile, no matter how lovely it looks at first, will eventually wear and chip off. The secret is to top your tile with a permanent, *penetrating* sealer, then protect it with several coats of a good floor polish.

You can use either a water-based or resinous sealer, and either a liquid acrylic finish or a paste wax polish. Ask the dealer what the manufacturer recommends, or find a janitorial supplier who takes care of the same kind of tile at a commercial establishment and ask him or her.

Just be sure never to let the polish wear down to the sealer; keep applying polish to those traffic paths. Daily maintenance of a tile floor is the same as for any other hard floor.

Coping with concrete floors

Dust-mopping concrete floors is a trick most of us haven't heard of. Concrete floors, believe it or not, are almost equal in square footage to carpet in many American homes. Unfinished full basements are common.

They wait many years—"until we can afford to finish those two bedrooms and a family room in the basement." Two-car garages are also a mass of concrete flooring. Both of these areas bear a constant flow of traffic back and forth into the "finished" part of the house. Concrete absorbs and holds stains and marks and produces much destructive material (dirt, grit, sand, etc.), so it's responsible for more cleaning time than you might realize. The surface of concrete (which is made of sand, cement, lime, and additives) will perpetually "bleed" dust and grit, which if not cleaned up regularly eventually circulates through your house.

Go get your broom right now and sweep your basement or garage. Leave the pile of residue, and go back and sweep again just as carefully. The second pile will amaze you, as will the third if you sweep again. Because concrete is textured and porous and "bleeds," vacuuming it is really the only way to get it dustless, and after use, it will again be dusty. If you want to eliminate hundreds of hours of direct and indirect adverse results from concrete floors in your home, seal the concrete. You've walked on many a sealed floor in supermarkets, malls, stadiums, on ramps, around pools, etc. It looks like it's varnished. Sealed concrete is easy and practical to maintain and will last for years.

You can seal your own concrete floors

Concrete has to cure at least twenty-eight days after pouring before it's ready to seal. It's best to seal it before it's used, because oil stains and other fluids may penetrate and will be difficult or impossible to remove, and

the seal will magnify any pre-existing marks.

On either old or new concrete, sweep up all surface dirt and remove everything possible from the floor (furniture, tools, etc.). Mop on a solution of strong alkaline cleaner, or better still, etching acid diluted in water. (Your janitorial supply house or paint store will have these.) Let it soak in awhile. It will break and release the lime and debris on the surface of the concrete, leaving a good firm clean base. If the floor is old and marked, scrub it with a floor machine (or your trusty hand floor scrubber). Even if you don't scrub, apply the solution and let it set. Then flush the solution off, using your floor squeegee. Rinse with a hose. Allow the floor to dry for five or more hours.

Transparent concrete seal or all-purpose seal can be obtained at paint stores or janitorial supply houses. (I've even used a gym-floor finish in two of my houses.) The new water-based concrete seals are wonderful! Apply the seal, according to directions, with any applicator that will distribute it in a nice thin even coat, and let it dry. Most concrete seals are self-leveling so it should turn out okay, but I'd advise a second coat to make sure all the "etched," rough surfaces are filled. (Don't try to save the used applicator. It isn't worth cleaning out.)

Once the seal is dry, you have a shiny, glossy, smooth (not slick) surface that can be waxed and maintained just like any hard floor. Stains, oil spills, etc., can be wiped off without leaving the usual ugly penetrating mark. Sealed concrete finish wears well. Chips and scrapes can be touched up with a small paintbrush or cloth.

Wood floors

Homeowners are in awe of their wood floors; literally thousands of them have written or called me, afraid they might hurt their wood. I assure you, wood floors are as durable as any other surface—including vinyl and cement—as long as they're properly finished and maintained.

Keep wooden floors covered with a protective polyurethane or resinous floor finish. If moisture penetrates wood it swells and pops off the finish; then the wood deteriorates rapidly.

Keep a good varnish or polyurethane finish on your wood floor, or follow the dealer's recommendations. Moisture won't bother wood if a finish repels it. However, once water or moisture gets into wood, it swells the grain and pops off the finish; then the wood deteriorates rapidly. Most wood floors can be treated like any other hard-surfaced floor if the surface finish is adequate, but use water sparingly. Be sure to apply a couple of coats of wax over the varnish or polyurethane; this protects the finish and makes the floor easy to clean.

Shy away from sanding wood floors except as a last resort. An eighth of an inch of wood taken off a ¾-inch floor really affects its performance. Cracks, crowns, and cupping will appear and squeaks will develop.

Sometimes, especially if you're rehabbing a much-abused old house, you'll have no choice but to sand down the floors. But chances are, if your wood floors are old- and ugly-looking, the problem's not the wood, but the layers of yellowed, cracked finish. If you sand it down, the old finish will gum up the belts of the sander, and it will be a mess. Plus, you'll be losing part of your floor. Instead, try this easy way: Buy a gallon or two of varnish or paint remover and apply it generously to the floor. The old varnish will instantly crumble and release its hold on the wood. Scrape it well, then use your trusty floor squeegee and dustpan to pick up the mess and get rid of it. This should leave the floor bare. If some old varnish does remain, use a little more remover and scrape some more; it will come off.

Without leaving water on the floor for too long, clean it as previously instructed (pages 75-79). This cleaning will get rid of any stripper residue; if it's not completely removed, future varnish applications will be adversely affected. Let the floor dry for ten hours or until any swelling is gone. Touch up with a sanding disc or a little hand-sanding if there's a nick or two. I'd ignore small cracks and marks; the seal you apply will blend things in. But if you want to remove all nicks and dents, use a floor machine with a flat sanding screen. Apply one coat of penetrating "seal"—thin it down so it will soak into the wood—and then one or two coats of varnish or polyurethane finish, the number of coats depending on the condition of the floor. Soft or cracked wood generally needs two coats to achieve a good gloss.

You won't believe how good your floor will look or how easy the job will be. Just be sure to read all the directions that come with floor care products, and don't be afraid to ask the dealer questions.

After a week or so, wax your pretty new floor—and dust-mop it daily thereafter.

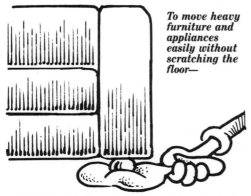

To move heavy furniture and appliances easily without scratching the floor—

A thick towel slipped under each leg will help the unit slide for easy cleaning access.

Remember daily maintenance for protection

After you've expended all the time and effort to get your floors clean and shiny, keep them clean daily and they'll last for years. Remember, it's the spills, crumbs, sand, dust, etc., that create the conditions that make you work. If a few black marks get on the floor, they'll be on top of the wax, and easily removed with the moist nylon cleaning pad on the end of your hand floor scrubber. The most efficient way to keep hard floors clean is to dust-mop them daily. Brooms stir up dust all over the place and leave fine unseen particles that will be ground into your new wax and eventually destroy the finish. A good dust mop is much faster and does a much better job than a broom. There's no comparison, especially if you have a good-quality commercial dust mop with a full-circle swivel head. It will cover a lot of ground quickly and is flat enough to get under furniture. It will gather gravel, paper clips, gum wrappers, safety pins, and the hundred other items that find their way to the floor, and will pick up and hold the dust. A dust mop is unbelievably effective on sealed concrete basement and garage floors, especially if it's treated to pick up dust.

Dust mop

Get dust and dirt off the floor regularly—preferably with a dust mop.

A 12-14" commercial-quality dust mop will pay you dividends. It cleans hard-surfaced floors better and faster than any broom.

The care and feeding of dust mops

You can treat your dust mop by spraying the head with a little Endust, furniture polish, or commercial dust mop treatment, or by taking the head off the frame and pouring a few tablespoonfuls of furniture polish into the pocket. Let it sit overnight (at least twelve hours) before mopping.

When you mop, use "s" strokes and keep the mop in contact with the floor, but don't bear down on it; pressure isn't necessary. The mop will turn and swivel under furniture (one of the advantages of a professional-quality mop). Mop next to the baseboard last.

Thoroughly shake out your mop after every use, preferably not over your neighbor's fence. When it gets full of dirt, vacuum it. When it gets stiff and smelly, launder it and re-treat. Never store your mop face down on cement or wood—all the treatment will soak out.

If you have only a small amount of hard flooring, do it by hand with a cleaning cloth (see Chapter 14) or dustcloth. You won't need a commercial dust mop.

Damp-mopping

Damp-mopping floors on a daily basis is fast and easy. Just fill the mop bucket half full of warm water and put in a little neutral cleaner. Follow the instructions on the label; if you get the cleaning solution too strong, it might "cut" or cloud the wax or finish. Dip your mop or sponge mop, wring or squeeze it slightly—leaving the mop head damp—and mop in a figure-eight pattern.

The floor of the average bathroom is so small it's not worth carrying a mop and bucket into such close quarters. Do it in one minute with your spray bottle of disinfectant cleaner and trusty cleaning cloth (see Chapter 12).

A quick review of floor care

VINYL TILE OR LINOLEUM

All vinyl, asphalt, and even "no-wax" floors must have a coat of wax or polish applied so that dirt and debris from foot traffic won't damage them. Keep such floors dust-mopped and damp-mopped regularly, even if "they don't look dirty." Damp-mop with a light neutral cleaner solution when soiled; rewax regularly in the traffic patterns.

WOOD

Make sure wood floors are sealed with a good resinous or polyurethane "membrane" finish so moisture and stains won't penetrate the wood. Then treat wood floors like any hard flooring. Wax, sweep, dust-mop and damp-mop to maintain, but go light on the water and don't let it puddle on the surface.

A few final words about floors

Remember, good matting at exterior and interior entrances will save you more floor work than all the gimmicks, tips, and miracle floor formulas combined. Avoid "one-stroke" miracle combinations that clean and wax your floor at the same time. And if anyone in the family has shoes or other footwear that leave black marks, I'd make a quick Salvation Army donation of them (the shoes, not the person!).

Some floors are much easier to maintain than others, so don't break your neck trying to match your neighbor's shine. Some floor material, because it's cheap, damaged, porous, discolored, or just plain ugly, is almost impossible to make look good. When you're putting in new flooring, stick to tested, reliable surfaces.

Some floors need three or four coats of wax to build them up to a gloss. A good shine will hide a multitude of sins. If a floor won't shine, or is difficult to maintain, consider replacing it or carpeting it if the lack of shine bothers you.

Pick a good-quality flooring. Remember that solid colors are tougher to maintain and keep looking good. Try to avoid flooring with grooves and indentations—it's literally the "pits." Smooth-surfaced floors are nicer—and much easier to keep clean.

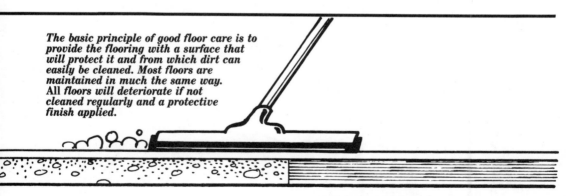

The basic principle of good floor care is to provide the flooring with a surface that will protect it and from which dirt can easily be cleaned. Most floors are maintained in much the same way. All floors will deteriorate if not cleaned regularly and a protective finish applied.

CONCRETE

Concrete will "bleed" dust and sand with use and when it's swept. Once interior concrete has cured, it should be cleaned thoroughly, let dry, and then sealed with a resinous or water-based concrete seal. The resulting protective finish lets it be maintained like other floors. Never paint concrete floors, because most paints will peel and chip off concrete.

STONE, BRICK, CERAMIC OR QUARRY TILE

The dozens of types of tiles available make it difficult to recommend a single method. Ask the dealer (or your local janitorial supply store) for a penetrating seal appropriate for your kind of tile. This will give the tile a base on which you can then apply a wax or acrylic finish. Remember that tiles intended to have a highly textured or "rustic" look will never shine no matter what—so don't waste your time and energy.

10.

How to clean carpets for a softer life

"Never shampoo a carpet before you have to, because once you do, it will get dirty faster" (Old Wives' Tales, cont'd). That's like saying, "Never wash your socks after the first wearing, because they'll get dirty faster." There are plenty of soothsayers around quoting great carpet wisdom to the homemaker, most of which costs you time and money. With some simple professional techniques, you can get the job done, keep your carpets looking sharp, and minimize your maintenance time. My company cleans and maintains several million square feet of carpet every night. What I've learned in the process applies to household as well as commercial carpet.

Buy quality carpet

Most of the carpet on the market is pretty good, but remember, it costs only a few dollars more to go first class. Pay the few extra dollars per yard to get the better grade, and have it installed professionally. You'll get thousands of dollars of benefit in comfort, durability, enjoyment, and ease of maintenance. Choose what you like, but make sure you get good stuff. Personally, for homes, I love deep nylon pile.

Selecting carpet color, style, and material is generally a personal privilege, but living with it (especially maintaining it) may not be a "privilege" if you don't choose wisely. For example, commercial carpets are so tightly woven and low-pile they're now referred to as "soft floors," not carpeted floors. Don't get too commercial-minded and buy the "wear like iron" commercial-style carpet.

Believe me, it *feels* like iron when you roll around on it playing with the kids or tackle a "living room floor" project. The feel and the looks are a large part of the value of home carpeting. Much low-pile or indoor-outdoor carpet is difficult to maintain, not because it gets any dirtier than a thicker, plusher carpet, but because of its short pile and the solid colors it usually comes in. Every tiny piece of litter or trash is highly visible on it, and little bits of thread and similar material resist being vacuumed off it; a good thick pile or shag can tolerate, undetected, just about anything from crumbs to catcher's mitts. There's nothing wrong with letting your rug help you out a little—as long as it isn't physically destructive to the carpet.

A homemaker will often spend hours selecting an exact shade, not realizing that, because of use, lighting, and depreciation, the color won't be the same as the color you chose for even a tenth of the time the carpet is in service. Color is one area where you should be cautious.

There's no way you can keep airborne soilants from industrial burning, home heating gases, family cooking, or foot-borne street oils, etc., from any carpet. All carpets will get soiled with time. Light golds, yellows, whites, and light pastel shades or flecks will serve you well if you live "el plusho" and your house is only a showplace. However, if you have children, grandchildren, animals, or home-study groups, those elegant light carpets will be a disaster. Light solid colors show soil and are difficult to shampoo, and often show "cow trails." Patterns and textures tend to hide soiling and wear.

Use common sense when you choose carpeting. Think of the

maintenance. Deep pile is harder to vacuum than medium pile. Although the old standby, wool, is lovely, I'd choose nylon, a synthetic, ten times over for stain resistance, wear, and cleanability. Oriental, Indian, and woven rugs must *always* be cleaned professionally. These and other area rugs *cause* housework: Area rugs present two surfaces (instead of one) to clean. They're always being kicked and wrinkled and they're easy to trip over. But they *are* beautiful. If you have to have them, hang them on a wall.

Kitchen and bathroom carpet

It all depends on your personal use and on the density and quality of the carpet: Nevertheless, I'd *never* have carpet in a bathroom. There is a 100 percent chance that moisture (new and used) will get on the carpet, as will hair spray and other grooming residue. It will stink, harbor germs, and look ugly. Bathroom carpeting takes much more time to care for than hard-surfaced flooring, and it deteriorates rapidly. Don't do it!

And in the kitchen? Where bread always falls jelly/mayonnaise/salami side down? Where meat juices run over the edge of the counter and dirty dishwater splashes out of the sink? Where pressure cookers of potato chowder explode and casseroles of baked beans are dropped? Don't you have better things to do than clean carpet?

High abuse areas such as bathrooms, kitchens, garages, and studios or workshops should have the lowest-maintenance, easiest-to-clean flooring possible. It will certainly save you time and grief, and probably money as well.

Regular maintenance is important

Carpet in a home or lightly trafficked commercial area is easier to take care of than a hardwood floor if it's maintained properly. Its biggest problem is neglect. A carpet that looks okay is often used and abused, going unnoticed until it's too late. Then the owner of the neglected carpet says, "Huh, I wonder why the fur is all falling out?" or "I can't remember what color it used to be. It must be time to clean it." At this stage most people wake up to the fact that carpets have to be maintained. But by then it's too late. Cleanup attempts are generally futile, and the owner becomes displeased with the carpet, unjustly blaming the problems on the salesperson or manufacturer.

You might think that carpet wear and damage result only from foot traffic. Wrong! Excessive carpet damage or wear results from a combination of foot traffic, furniture "pressure," and residues (such as sand and grit) that are allowed to remain in the carpet. Any sharp, abrasive particles or articles on or at the base of the carpet fibers are, as the carpet is walked on, ground against each other and in time, the fibers that aren't cut or damaged are soiled. The carpet wears out and gets soiled from the bottom as well as the top. Thus, to maintain your carpet properly, you've got to keep off or remove surface litter, dust, grit, wet soils, and the old airborne soils before they become embedded in your carpet. Another reminder: Good matting will eliminate a big share of this, especially wet soils and grit. Airborne dust you have to live with. Litter you can pick up or vacuum. The real culprit is embedded dirt.

Which vacuum?

Vacuum cleaners were invented to get surface dust, embedded dirt, and litter from carpets efficiently. Few vacuums make as much impression on the carpet as they do on the user who thinks noise, chrome, and suction are the ultimate. For ages, vacuum salespeople (all equal in wind velocity to their products) have unloaded shiny, overpriced machines on customers fascinated by suction and attachments. Neither of these is that important in maintaining your carpet and saving yourself housecleaning hours. After showing you how a vacuum can do everything but brush your teeth, the sales approach is to drop a steel ball on the floor and suck it up into the vacuum. The gullible potential customer thinks, "If that vacuum can get a big steel ball off the carpet, sand and gravel will be a snap!"

Wrong! First, the steel ball trick is a volume maneuver that any vacuum, weak or strong, old or new, can do under the right conditions. Just get a

steel ball slightly smaller than the hose and the ball is easily slurped up. Now take a piece of thread and mash it onto the carpet so it has a little static bind. A vacuum cleaner strong enough to pick up a piano bench will often have trouble picking up the thread because there's no "displacement lift." We've all tried to get up a thread, haven't we? Likewise, suction alone won't remove the embedded particles of dirt, grit, and sand. It will remove only the surface soil because, as with the thread, the displacement lift isn't there and the carpet fibers are standing in the way to effectively hold the embedded dirt and grit, and all those other villains grinding away at your carpet. A good "beater brush" vacuum is what's needed to pull those babies out of the pile.

Beat it!

The beater brush, or beater bar, vacuum's distinguishing feature is a rapidly rotating brush that beats, combs, and vibrates the carpet. This loosens and dislodges embedded dirt and soil so the suction can pull it up into the vacuum. Most beater brush heads will adjust to different heights and won't wear out carpet under normal use.

Rugs and carpets must have good daily care with a beater-brush-type vacuum to keep dirt out of the roots.

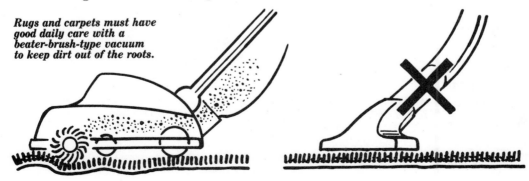

Don't abuse your vacuum

Eighty percent of vacuuming problems are caused not by a loose nut on the machine, but by the loose nut running it. The personality and habits of the user can take a great toll on vacuums. For example, I gave two heavy-duty commercial vacuum cleaners for Christmas in 1965, one to my mother-in-law and one to another relative. My mother-in-law's vacuum still works like new and she has used it daily for the past thirteen years. The other one lasted less than thirteen months.

The unintentional (or sometimes intentional) vacuuming of coat hangers, Scout badges, marbles, overshoes, and scissors is what hurts vacuums. That sickening knock, knock, knock you hear when the vacuum picks up one of these or similar articles generally means the (usually plastic) blades of the little gizmo that generates suction, called the impeller or the turbulator fan, are being sheared off. If you're vacuuming more and enjoying it less (getting up less dirt), you had probably better replace the fan. It's not uncommon to have a fine-running vacuum without suction, and a beat-up $5 fan is generally the reason. (If it's not the fan, then it's probably the beater brush.)

Note: A strong bar magnet screw-mounted to the front of your upright vacuum will pick up tacks, pins, needles, scissors, can openers, or any other metal object you might miss before vacuuming. It will save injuries to crawling babies, wrestling kids, and nice, new vacuum cleaners.

Are you the one in seven?

National studies show that one out of every seven homemakers needs a new vacuum cleaner. If you're that one, get it before your spouse spends the money on a new router or a fancy new computer program he'll use just once or twice during the rest of his life.

There are exceptions that might require an "exceptional" vacuum cleaner, but in 99 percent of the cases the market has just what you need. The ideal? I would buy two vacuums: first, an upright beater-brush type. (I hate canister-type vacuums that drag behind you like a ball and chain.) Go a step further and get a commercial upright. These are almost like the regular model sold downtown—except they generally have a longer cord, a heavy-duty beater bar, a more durable turn-on switch, and a better-quality bag. Just be sure you choose a model you feel comfortable handling. Cloth bags are usually preferable: Paper filter replacement bags are costly to buy and a nuisance to store. (An interesting exception, where paper disposables are an advantage, is in a tropical climate, where there are bugs, lizards, ants—and other creatures great and small—capable of hiding in deep shag. Their condition after passing through the beater bar and fan blades is such that a cloth bag is soon befouled.)

If you use doormats efficiently, you'll cut down vacuuming intake considerably, and a cloth bag will last a long time. Cloth bags need to be emptied *before* they're a third full and shaken well to keep them from becoming impregnated with soil. If you lack a suitable alley, north forty, or yard to do the airing, disposable bags might serve you better. When bags get too clogged, you'll smell dust when you click the vacuum on. If you see dust pouring out when you start the vacuum up, you've waited too long.

There are some pretty good upright vacuums on the market. In the buildings we clean professionally all over the U.S., we use Eurekas, Kirbys, Hoovers, Royals, Advances, Clarkes, and others. They all work fine if maintained properly. People either love or hate their vacuums beyond all reason, so I never try to switch a Kirby lover to a Eureka or a Hoover. You should be able to buy a first-class commercial upright for $150-$200.

Resist buying a boxful of extra attachments that do everything from painting to pan-frying. Most of them are trinkets, and gradually the gadget accessories break or get lost and eventually the machine is only used for what you needed it for in the first place—to vacuum! Ninety-five percent of your vacuuming can be accomplished with just two or three basic tools.

My criticism of attachments is well documented by your own experience. That big display box of nickel-plated gizmos to hook up to your vacuum is a dandy selling point, but it's shuffled, unused, from closet to closet for years until the box disintegrates. Then the tools themselves are banged around but never used. Finally, after twelve years, you need the goose-necked anteater attachment to vacuum the glove box of the car. Then you can't find it! Don't buy them.

Just get a sturdy, simple upright. Do be sure to get a vacuum with a long cord—who among us has not wished a hundred times that the vacuum cord was "just ten feet longer"? An extension cord is a pain and cuts your efficiency greatly. Every time you need to use it you have to hunt it down from the family member who borrowed it for some other purpose.

For your second machine, invest in a tank-type wet-dry vacuum. You'll be money and time ahead.

The wet-dry vacuum

A wet-dry is a vacuum that can be safely used to pick up both dry material and liquids. Generally this is accomplished by a simple filter adjustment. Wet-drys are great! They are the vacuums to buy a few attachments for, and the first one should be an extra-long hose.

A 5-gallon or smaller wet-dry is fine for household use. They range in price from $65 at Sears or K-Mart to $500. For around $300, you should be able to obtain a beautiful commercial unit that will last for years—if your neighbors or relatives don't find out about it. When they do, your efficient little wet-dry will be cleaning carpet spills, spots, car upholstery, floors, furniture, drapes, rafters (another reason for a long hose), carpet edges, campers, boats . . . the list could go on, take my word for it.

The upright and wet-dry vacuums together are approximately a $500 investment and will cover all your vacuum needs, plus a few dozen more you never knew you had.

Built-in vacuum systems

My first experience with a built-in vacuum came when I opened a closet in a house we were cleaning. I winced in startled fright at what I thought was a giant coiled python ready to strike. Its sedate reaction identified it as the longest vacuum hose I'd ever seen. "Wow, there must be some hunk of a vacuum to fit this baby," I thought. The owner later showed me the little wall receptacle where the hose inserted and turned into an instant vacuum. I then thought the central vacuum was a novelty for the rich and weird, and in the next year or so saw or heard of only a few more—though all of their owners seemed to be in love with them.

As I met ever more homemakers across the nation in my seminars and tours, "What about a central vacuum?" was asked at almost every stop. I then began an aggressive hunt for sources of the central vacuum and found my builder and supplier were as uneducated as I was. I have since located lots of sources and the more I found out about them the more enthusiastic I became. I am now putting one in my new maintenance-free home and adapting one in my twenty-year-old home. Though they cost between $400 and $900 to put in, that's a bargain considering the time and energy they will save if you can afford them. (If you can't find a source, write to Housework, P.O. Box 39, Pocatello, ID 83204, and I'll send you a sheet of names.)

The hose of one of these is a little awkward at first if it's too long; I'd put in a few more receptacles so you can use a short hose. Once in a while you need beater brush action to bounce dirt out, so the manufacturers do make a beater-brush head for the hose.

Be sure to put a couple of outlets in the garage and on the stair areas. Here are the pluses of the central vacuum system:

1. *It saves wear and tear on the house (the vacuum hitting furniture legs and baseboards, etc.).*

2. *It's the cleanest vacuum going. Residual dust has no home here—it goes out of the room.*

3. *Amazing—it's quiet—since the motor's in the basement or garage, far away. No noise.*

4. *Since all you're handling is a light hose, it's super easy to use, especially for those once-a-day pickups or once-overs.*

But the nicest thing about central vacuums is their simplicity—no canister to drag around, no cord to keep flipping over furniture (or pulling out of the socket). Central vacuums also have *lots* of power, so don't go sticking it on your skin to test the suction.

A vacuuming in time. . . .

A good carpet-cleaning program will free you from hours of work and emotional anguish. Clean carpets look and feel better, and they last longer. A regularly maintained carpet means less frequent shampooing, less time expended on carpet care, a longer life for the carpet, and more compliments from your guests!

The ideal carpet care plan is to (1) keep all possible dust, dirt, and abrasive material from getting on the carpet—the job of good matting; (2) regularly remove all litter and extract harmful embedded debris from the carpet—the job of a good vacuum; (3) keep grime cleaned off the top of the carpet so that it doesn't have a chance to penetrate—the job of effective surface cleaning.

Install a good set of mats as explained in Chapter 8, and vacuum carpets and mats regularly. Don't wait until you can see the dirt. Just because it's possible to camouflage crumbs, dog biscuits, pins, pennies, and peelings in a big luxurious shag doesn't mean you should overdo it. All materials detrimental to carpeting should be kept out of the carpet. I've seen homes go from eight to ten years before the carpets needed shampooing, all because of good matting and regular maintenance. Avoiding unnecessary shampooing is wise because shampooing is expensive, whether you do it yourself or have it done professionally.

Carpeted stairways don't have to be a pain to keep clean. I've found the easy way to keep stairs and corners vacuumed is to pick up your upright and vacuum the tread so the beater brush can get the embedded dirt. Then, every few weeks, months, or even once a year, get a damp cloth and wipe the corners out; the corners don't get that dirty and won't be depreciated by wear because there's no wear on them. You can also take a tank-type vacuum with a long hose and an upholstery attachment and use vigorous hand action on your stairs.

Vacuum carpeted stairways regularly; the corners only need to be wiped with a damp cloth occasionally.

The edges of wall-to-wall carpet can be approached this way, too—either wiped with a damp cloth from time to time, swept with a broom, or vacuumed with a hand tool.

Edges are only a visual problem because traffic wear is impossible.

Sweep when they're dusty.

Always keep your vacuum on carpeted area while it's running. I've ruined a beautiful wood floor by running a low-adjusted beater-bar vacuum over it. The metal part of the bar thumped the floor on every rotation and dented it (at great expense to me, since our insurance covers liability but not stupidity).

Check out your vacuum regularly. It's one of your most important household tools. The biggest secret of efficient vacuuming is *keeping your vacuum well maintained.* Keep cloth bags emptied and shaken out so the pores in the cloth won't get clogged. Check, and if necessary, replace the beater brush when it starts to wear. Make sure the cord, the impeller or

Never feel under a beater vacuum to see if it's working.

turbulator fan, and the belts are all in good shape; if any one of these items isn't working at top form, your vacuum function is impaired.

Make sure the beater and belt are functioning properly.

WRONG!
Kicks dirt out and away from vacuum.

RIGHT!
Pulls dirt under vacuum to the intake.

Spots and stains

For spot and stain removal, I've gathered the opinions of many experts, homemakers, and carpet manufacturers to construct an effective home approach. This approach, plus a guide to dealing with specific stains, is located at the end of this chapter.

Soil retardant

It's generally a good idea to treat carpet with soil retardant.

A soil retardant is a chemical treatment that helps carpet resist soiling and helps prevent water- and soil-based spots and spills from becoming hard-to-remove stains. Water-based soiling agents especially, such as soft drinks, milk, coffee, tea, mud, and winter slush, cause big maintenance problems because they soak into carpet fibers and backing and rapidly deteriorate appearance.

Soil retardants can be applied to *clean* carpeting, old or new. (It's generally applied at the mill during manufacture, so chances are your new carpet has it. Ask, when you're purchasing a carpet.)

The best-known brand of soil retardant is Scotchgard, made by the 3M Company. If applied correctly, it can be a real boon. After spending time in the 3M testing labs observing control blocks of carpet, treated and untreated, I was impressed. You can apply Scotchgard yourself following the directions on the container, or you can have your dealer do it for you. You can even purchase carpet and upholstery shampoo containing Scotchgard!

But just because carpet is protected by a soil retardant doesn't mean you can relax. You must still keep up your regular schedule of carpet cleaning and maintenance. Your carpets will last much longer and look much better. Remember, when you start noticing that your carpets look bad, it's too late!

Anti-static agents

Static electricity is the mild shock produced when you touch a metal object after walking across a carpet. It's the result of friction. While not harmful—unless you have a home computer that will go on the blink—it can be irritating. And static electricity can actually pull dust particles from the air. By eliminating static, you keep your carpet cleaner.

Some carpeting contains a small amount of stainless steel fiber to dissipate static electricity. For carpeting that lacks this feature, applying an anti-static agent to the carpet periodically can help the problem.

Shampooing the carpet

If your carpets haven't had proper maintenance, and you think they're too far gone, a major cleaning, washing, or, as most call it, "shampooing," is needed. There are several ways to determine when that shampooing is needed:

1. *Carpet is matted and sticky.*

2. *You can't remember its real color. Check out a saved remnant. Many carpets soil and darken so gradually you don't realize it's*

happening. (Remember, of course, that every carpet loses some color by fading, age, and daily wear and tear. And shampooing only cleans carpet; it doesn't restore color and body.)

3. *You can see a three-foot grimy circle around the TV chair.*

4. *A dust storm follows when you walk across it!*

You have two basic choices to get the job done: Do it yourself or call a professional. And once it's clean, start a bonnet program (pages 92-93).

I'm the first to push independence and "doing your own thing," but I caution you about the pitfalls of shampooing your own carpet. It's not necessarily a complicated job, but don't be deceived by the propaganda of trouble-free, money-saving, automatic, do-it-all machinery. The operator of the machine has to have some knowledge, the ability to adapt to different carpet-cleaning requirements, and understand how much moisture and chemical to use, or else a poor cleaning job, overwetting, or fiber and backing damage will result. It amazes me that people will spend $2,500 for a carpet, then attack it with powerful cleaning gear without any experience whatsoever.

Another pitfall is cost-value miscalculation. Take, for example, a 14x20-foot living room carpet, which a professional might do for $30. A pair of homeowners (one of whom is missing a fishing trip) will drive ten miles across town to rent a big steamer or rug outfit for $15. Then they'll buy $5 worth of chemicals, skin up the family car getting it all in, and drive another ten miles home. They'll unload the heavy equipment, grunting and

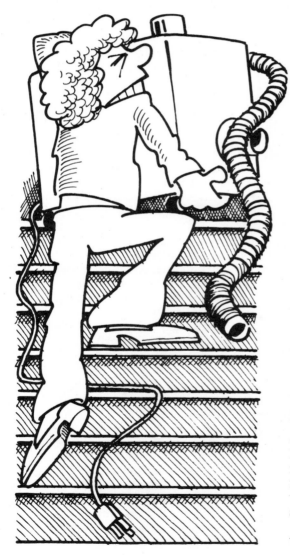

groaning. Then they'll move furniture, read directions, spend most of Saturday cleaning carpet, and probably will have to drive back for more shampoo. The results will be questionable.

Once they're finished, it's a repeat performance of loading and driving to return the equipment. At the end of the day, they've spent $35 on gas, rent, shampoo, etc.—not to mention their time; they are dead tired; have experienced a smashed hand, three arguments, two dogfights—and come Sunday night the carpet still isn't dry in places. I've cleaned carpets for twenty years, and always do my own because I know how and have easy access to the equipment, but I would never do my own if I had to round up and rent the mediocre machines available and go through all that. I couldn't afford it and wouldn't enjoy the hassle.

If you insist on doing it yourself, remember that rental "steam" extraction units generally won't clean carpets well by themselves. Rotary motion or scrubbing action with shampoo should be applied to the carpet by hand or machine to loosen and deep-clean it. This should be followed by rinsing or "extracting" with plain hot water to remove all dirt, soap, etc. Caution should be taken not to over-wet the carpet or drive dirt deeper into the nap; vacuum well before shampooing, and make sure you don't let the cleaning solution sit too long before you extract it. If the carpet is long-napped it will sometimes be necessary to rake or sweep the carpet to a stand-up position to dry after shampooing.

Then again, there are also pitfalls to having your carpet done. Not all so-called professionals *are* professionals. Some "carpet cleaners" are opportunists who were franchised or hired for a big kill; their training has been by trial and error. The method used in shampooing carpets is important. That TV before-and-after demonstration of a great contrast once a little foamy carpet shampoo is rubbed on is deceptive. That isn't cleanliness you behold, but the "optical brightening" most carpets exhibit when wetted. After a light foam job, many carpets appear to gleam and sparkle, but they can still be filthy.

This has been the story with most home carpet cleaning and is in fact the reason you so often hear: "Never shampoo your carpets, for once you do, they will get dirty faster." They *do* get dirty faster, but only because the surface was grazed with a dab of shampoo, and the dirt and soap was carried by the moisture down to the bottom of the fibers, only to emerge quickly when the carpet is in use again. (Remember—ask yourself, when you

clean, where the dirt goes. If you can't figure it out, the dirt probably isn't coming out.) Also, many shampoos leave a soil-attracting residue on the carpet fibers.

Protect carpet when shampooing. Block furniture legs with pieces of cardboard or waxed paper.

If an imprint remains . . .

Rub the area with a bit of clear water.

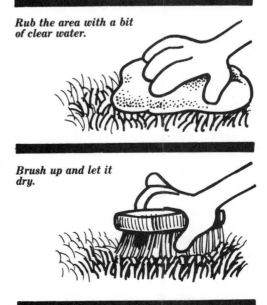

Brush up and let it dry.

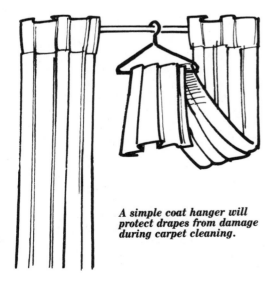

A simple coat hanger will protect drapes from damage during carpet cleaning.

Great deals?

You will be approached by mail or by phone with the "mist" method, the "dry foam" method, the "liquid" method, the "dry powder" method, and the latest, the "steam" method. I would be cautious of any of these on my carpets because they are all in some way obsolete or ineffective. For example, "steam" isn't what it's cracked up to be, but when steam cleaning hit the market, it positively revolutionized carpet cleaning. It wasn't the steam itself but the extraction process that was so valuable: Hot cleaning solution is pressure-injected into the carpet, and a super-strong wet vacuum is used immediately to pull almost all the moisture back out.

It's my opinion that steam extraction alone generally won't clean an old, dirty carpet. I know the water extracted from the carpet is impressively muddy, but remember that the dwell time between the solution's being injected and removed is so brief that it can't dissolve much of the goop adhering to the fibers. Rotary motion or scrubbing action is needed after the solution is applied to loosen all the dirt and deep-clean the carpet. This should be followed by extracting (rinsing) to remove all dirt, soap, etc.

If you do decide to have your carpets done rather than do them yourself, first make sure there's a good, professional carpet cleaner in your area. (*Always check references.*) They'll do a better job than you can, and probably save you money over doing it yourself.

Be sure to get a firm price quote. And ask which method they use. If they say "steam" or "extraction," request a truck-mounted unit that heats the solution and has the power to actually steam-clean your carpet. Request that they pre-spot and pre-spray any stains.

If they say "rotary," make sure that after they've scrubbed the carpet it is rinsed with hot water by the extraction method. That means, if nine gallons of liquid go into the carpet, they get eight and a half gallons back out. Some professionals call the combination of rotary scrubbing and hot water extraction "showcase" cleaning. It's the most expensive but does the best job.

The bonnet system

One new method used with success commercially and now being adopted for home use is the spin-clean, or yarn bonnet, system.

The bonnet system is a surface-cleaning procedure in which the carpet is wiped or rubbed clean with a heavy cloth or toweling "bonnet." This is not to be mistaken for a deep-cleaning operation; it's a carpet-maintenance technique intended to never let carpet get to the point of needing major shampooing. The bonnet system is being used by most progressive commercial companies. I've been in a Bell System office in Pasadena, California, that has used this method for seven years. The carpets, even in the reception area, are clean and new-looking, though they've never been shampooed.

The bonnet treatment done twice monthly or more often in a home is fast, easy, and inexpensive. It's a good maintenance system that delays or precludes shampooing, and keeps carpets fresh and consistently clean.

Even if you do practice a good daily vacuuming program to prevent dirt from reaching and damaging the roots of the carpet, vacuuming can't remove grime that has soiled the surface of the carpet. But bonneting will, and it's simple.

A yarn pad or disk, two inches or so thick, is moistened with carpet-cleaning solution, wrung in your roller mop bucket, then mounted under a buffer (household floor polisher) and run over the carpet. The floor buffer moves the pad in a rotating motion on the carpet. The bonnet will pick up and absorb surface grime and soils. When the pad becomes dirty, it is turned over and the process is repeated. When both sides are dirty, the bonnet is rinsed clean in the mop bucket, wrung, and the process repeated again.

In a home, a once-a-month bonneting would be plenty. It does take a certain solution like Argo Sheen to produce best results, so check with a professional supplier if you plan to try the bonnet system. A janitorial supply house can direct you to the right chemical to clean with and a bonnet to fit your floor machine.

Although this is not presently a well-known system, it will be. I love it; any person who has used it loves it too. Small oscillating (like Square Buff) or orbiting machines will soon be feasible to own. A whole carpet-cleaning setup for your home and your relatives', machine and all, could be had for about $650. Most "household gimmick" machines aren't as fast and effective as a good commercial unit, which is why four or five neighbors or relatives might want to go in together on a pass-around unit.

I like the bonnet system because it holds carpets to a consistent level of cleanliness and replaces the old inefficient up-and-down approach to cleaning. There is something spiritually uplifting about a clean fresh expanse of carpet.

How to remove carpet stains

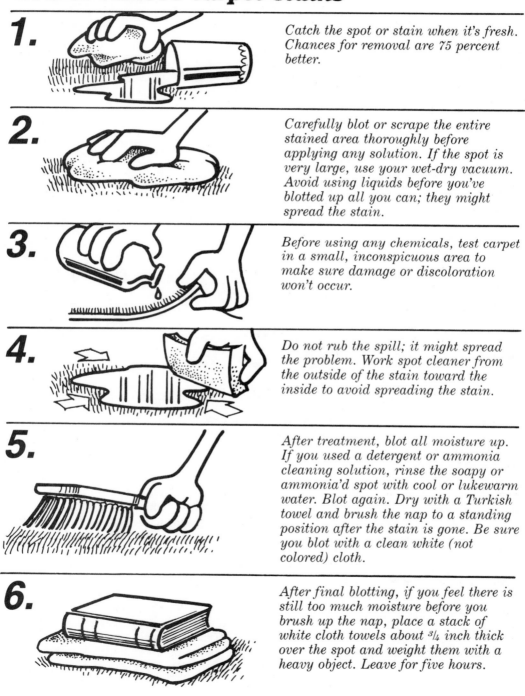

1. Catch the spot or stain when it's fresh. Chances for removal are 75 percent better.

2. Carefully blot or scrape the entire stained area thoroughly before applying any solution. If the spot is very large, use your wet-dry vacuum. Avoid using liquids before you've blotted up all you can; they might spread the stain.

3. Before using any chemicals, test carpet in a small, inconspicuous area to make sure damage or discoloration won't occur.

4. Do not rub the spill; it might spread the problem. Work spot cleaner from the outside of the stain toward the inside to avoid spreading the stain.

5. After treatment, blot all moisture up. If you used a detergent or ammonia cleaning solution, rinse the soapy or ammonia'd spot with cool or lukewarm water. Blot again. Dry with a Turkish towel and brush the nap to a standing position after the stain is gone. Be sure you blot with a clean white (not colored) cloth.

6. After final blotting, if you feel there is still too much moisture before you brush up the nap, place a stack of white cloth towels about ¾ inch thick over the spot and weight them with a heavy object. Leave for five hours.

Coping with Carpet Catastrophes

Carpet problems (spills, burns, spots, etc.) are just as upsetting in the home as they are in the commercial buildings I clean. A puddle of orange pop on your living room rug will panic you just as surely as a glaring coffee stain on the carpeting in front of a bank teller will turn off customers.

There are two basic approaches to take to spills:

One way is to keep just two different spot removers on hand: an all-purpose spotter for water-based substances (food, blood, etc.), and a solvent spotter for tar, grease, and oil stains. (If a particular problem keeps recurring in your household, you may want to select just an item or two from the spotting kit list below in addition to the two spotters and keep it on hand— some type of carpet deodorant, for example, if you have pet "accidents" or children in toilet training.) These spotters are available at janitorial supply houses, and are very effective; if there's a stain they won't remove, you can call in a professional to get the spot out chemically or to doughnut-cut that piece of carpet and plug in a new piece.

If you're a do-it-yourself type, keep the following spotting kit around and consult the stain chart below. A janitorial supply house will carry any of the items not available at the supermarket or discount store. Both the kit and chart are useful on upholstery and in the laundry room, too.

Complete Tools and Supplies

If you really want to be prepared for everything, keep the following items on hand to attack fresh spills on your carpets. Otherwise, get the two basic spotters above, pick the item or two from the following list that you'll use most, and use the chart below for reference.

- **Neutral dish detergent, i.e., one advertised as safe for fine fabrics, such as Trend, Vel, Dreft, or Ivory Liquid. Dilute 20:1 with water to use for spot removal.**
- **Common household ammonia— clear, sudsy, or lemon-scented. When using ammonia for spot removal, always dilute with 10 parts water.**
- **Nonflammable dry-cleaning fluid, such as Carbona, Renuzit, Energine, or "perk" (perchloroethylene, used by professional dry cleaners). Use straight from the container. Do not use gasoline, lighter fluid, or carbon tetrachloride.**
- **Denatured alcohol.**
- **Acetone (or non-oily nail polish remover). *Not* for use on acetate fibers.**
- **Hydrogen peroxide, 3-5% concentration.**
- **Protein digester enzyme treatment.**
- **Rust remover.**
- **Water-soluble deodorant or other type of odor eradicator.**
- **Distilled white vinegar. Dilute 50-50 with water.**
- **Clean white terry cloth towels.**
- **A soft-bristled nylon scrub brush.**
- **A spatula or putty knife.**
- **A wet-dry vacuum.**

Remember, keep cleaning solutions and tools safely out of reach of little children. I would suggest you store your spot removal tools and supplies in a small plastic hand carrying tray or "maid basket." This will organize your supplies for quick attack on spots.

It's important before you try to deal with it to know what a stain or mark on the carpet *is*. What base is it—water or oil? You must match the base of the stain to the base of the cleaner—for instance, a water-based detergent solution won't make much of an impact on oil, but a petroleum-based solvent spotter will dissolve it immediately.

Smelling and feeling a spot will help you determine what it is. You can also ask other household members (nicely) if they know anything about how the spot got there. If a spot is darker than the carpet, you have a chance of removing it; if it's lighter, that means the substance bleached the fibers and the spot will need to be plugged (unless you can rearrange the furniture).

Bleaching a stain—even with the relatively mild hydrogen peroxide—is a last resort, and I don't generally recommend it, unless you want a little adventure or a new conversation piece (spot). Before you bleach, *always* test the carpet or fabric in an unobtrusive place.

If you have wool carpet or upholstery, try to avoid wet-cleaning it. Use dry-cleaning solvents whenever possible. Call your dealer for advice.

Be patient—give the chemicals time to work. Don't expect all stains to come out immediately—most take some time.

Most old stains and spots can't be removed, so don't get your hopes up too high about that three-year-old cherry popsicle stain you've had the lamp table over. It might have to remain until you replace the rug!

Stain Removal Chart

STAIN/SPOT	METHOD
acids (bowl cleaner, drain cleaner, vinegar)	*Apply a solution of baking soda and water to neutralize the spot. (It's neutralized when the acid smell disappears.) Then apply ammonia solution and rinse with cold water.*
aloholic beverages	*Apply detergent solution; blot. Apply vinegar solution; blot. Apply ammonia solution; blot. Bleach with 3-5% hydrogen peroxide if necessary. Rinse with cold water; blot dry.*
Alkali (lye, concentrated ammonia, trisodium phosphate)	*Apply vinegar solution, then rinse and blot.*

STAIN/SPOT	METHOD
blood	*Scrape off surface. Apply cool detergent solution; blot. Apply cool ammonia solution; blot. Rinse; blot dry. Apply rust remover followed by 3-5% hydrogen peroxide if stain remains.*
butter, margarine	*Apply dry-cleaning solvent; blot. Apply detergent solution; blot. Rinse; blot dry.*
candle wax	*Scrape off surface. Place a cloth over stain and run a warm iron over it to melt and absorb the wax. Apply dry-cleaning solvent; blot. Repeat if necessary.*
candy	*Clean off with dull knife. Apply ammonia solution; blot. Apply neutral detergent solution; blot. Rinse. Blot.*
catsup, tomato sauce	*Apply cool detergent or ammonia solution; blot. If stain remains, apply 3-5% hydrogen peroxide. Rinse; blot dry.*
chewing gum	*If hard and solid, apply commercial aerosol gum freeze (ice cubes in a plastic bag will work sometimes) until the gum is brittle. Break into pieces and vacuum up. Apply dry-cleaning solvent to residue.*
chocolate	*Scrape off surface. Apply cool detergent solution; blot. Apply ammonia solution; blot. Apply vinegar solution; blot. Rinse; blot dry.*
cigarette burns	*If the burn is slight, rub with dry steel wool, or, if you feel confident, trim the tufts. If the burn is bad, have a professional "doughnut cut" the damaged area and plug a new piece in, or do it yourself.*
cleaners	*Rinse thoroughly with clear water until residue is gone. Blot dry.*
coffee	*Rub with a paste of raw egg yolk; rinse. If stain is old, apply a few drops of denatured alcohol; rinse.*
crayon	*Apply dry-cleaning solvent; blot. Apply detergent solution. Rinse; blot dry.*
food coloring/dyes	*Apply detergent solution, blotting frequently (a dried stain can easily spread when wet). Repeat until towel picks up no color. Apply ammonia solution; blot. Rinse; blot dry.*

STAIN/SPOT	METHOD
furniture polish	*Apply dry-cleaning solvent; blot. Apply detergent solution; blot. Rinse; blot dry. (If the polish is the "scratch cover" kind, the stain is almost impossible to remove completely if you don't catch it while fresh, so use a better dropcloth next time or do it in the basement or garage.)*
grass stains	*Apply acetone (but not to acetate fibers!); blot. Apply deter*gent solution; blot. Rinse; blot. Apply ammonia solution; blot. Apply vinegar solution; blot. Rinse; blot dry. If necessary, bleach with 3-5% hydrogen peroxide.
grease, oil	*Apply commercial petroleum solvent spotter, paint thinner, or "perk." Work to center to avoid ring. Blot. Apply light detergent solution; rinse.*
ink (ballpoint)	*Apply dry cleaning solvent; blot. Apply denatured alcohol; blot. Apply acetone. If stain remains, apply rust remover. Professional plugging or bleaching may be necessary.*
ink (felt-tip)	*Most felt-tip inks are water-soluble and easily cleaned. But if a pen is marked "permanent," they're right.*
ink (India)	*Apply dry-cleaning solvent. Apply detergent solution; blot. Apply ammonia solution; blot. Rinse; blot dry. (This stain is often permanent.)*
iodine, mercurochrome, Merthiolate	*Apply denatured alcohol; blot. Apply ammonia solution; blot. Rinse. (Some stain may remain.)*
jam, jelly	*Apply detergent solution; blot. Apply vinegar solution; blot. Rinse; blot dry.*
lipstick	*Scrpae off surface, taking care not to spread the stain. Apply dry-cleaning solvent; blot. Apply detergent solution; blot. Apply ammonia solution; blot. Apply vinegar solution; blot. Rinse; blot.*
mildew	*Apply solution of one teaspoon disinfectant cleaner to one cup water; blot. Apply ammonia solution; blot. Rinse; blot. Keep area dry!*
milk, cream, ice cream	*Apply ammonia solution or a protein digester; rinse. If area is large, shampoo afterward.*

STAIN/SPOT	METHOD
mud	*Allow to dry and brush or scrape off as much as possible. Apply detergent or ammonia solution; blot. Rinse; blot dry. If stain remains, apply dry-cleaning solvent; blot dry.*
mustard	*Apply detergent solution; blot. Apply vinegar solution; blot. If stain remains, apply rust remover or hydrogen peroxide solution; blot. Do not use ammonia or alkalies.*
nail polish	*Apply dry-cleaning solvent. Apply acetone. If stain remains, apply detergent solution; blot dry. Apply ammonia solution; blot. Apply vinegar solution; blot. Rinse; blot dry.*
odors	*Apply solution of one teaspoon disinfectant cleaner to one cup water. Follow with water-soluble deodorant. If an odor has permeated the carpet and the backing or mat, it is nearly impossible to get out. Ask a reliable carpet cleaner what they use or have them do it for you.*
paint (oil base)	*Check label on paint for specific thinner or solvent to use, or apply dry-cleaning solvent. If stain remains, cover it with towels dampened with dry-cleaning solvent or paint thinner to soften for several hours; blot with solvent. Apply several drops of detergent solution and work into the stain; blot. Apply ammonia solution; blot. Rinse with warm water; blot dry.*
paint (latex)	*Apply detergent solution; blot. Apply ammonia solution; blot. Rinse; blot. If a paint spill has dried, a little lacquer thinner will soften and remove it. (It could also melt the carpet, so test first.)*
rust	*Rub with steel wool, then apply commercial rust remover if necessary.*
shoe polish	*Apply dry-cleaning solvent. Apply detergent solution; blot. Apply ammonia solution; blot. Rinse; blot dry. If stain remains, bleaching with 3-5% hydrogen peroxide or professional plugging may be necessary.*
urine	*Blot up as much as possible. Apply detergent solution, then ammonia solution; blot. Apply vinegar solution; blot. Rinse; blot dry. If stain remains, apply rust remover; bleaching with 3-5% hydrogen peroxide might be necessary. (Urine stains may remove dye from fibers.) An odor eradicator may be necessary.*
vomit	*Blot up as much as possible. Apply detergent solution; blot. Apply ammonia solution; blot. Apply vinegar solution; blot. Rinse; blot dry.*

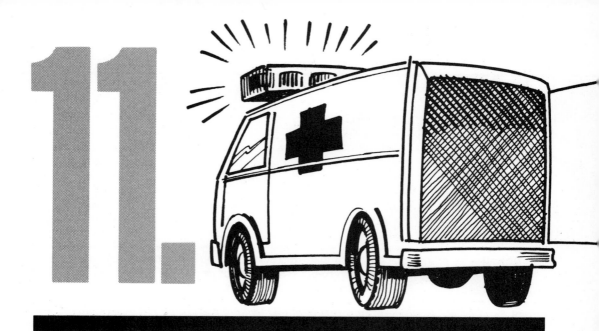

11.

What to do about furniture

"What should I do about furniture?" is a question I'm asked repeatedly by homemakers. As a male, my attitude toward furniture is, "I dislike moving it, and I dislike buying it even more." A woman has a finer appreciation for furniture because she's often the one who chooses it, plus much of her time is spent maintaining its appearance.

In an attempt to eliminate both my furniture frustrations, I designed most of the furniture out of a home we built in the resort mountains of Sun Valley, Idaho. Our living room had an octagonal conversation pit padded with vinyl-backed cushions. Twelve or thirteen people could sit and visit comfortably. A plush padded two-stair landing where ten or twelve more visitors could sit faced into the living room. This house didn't have a single piece of furniture except for the beds and the dining room set. I built the stereo and bookcases in, to eliminate cabinets and stands. Pedestal beds were built to the floor and other such adjustments were made to eliminate the clutter and upkeep of furniture. Our home was not only beautiful but usable for family and groups of up to forty, and I didn't have to buy

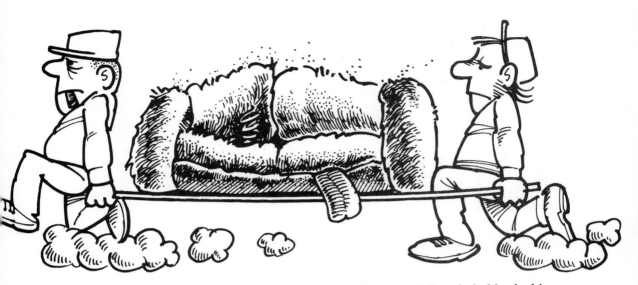

furniture or move it!

But for most of you, furniture not only must be bought and moved, it must be cleaned. So the question becomes, "How do I keep my furniture looking nice without a lot of time and effort?"

Attempts to answer this question have greatly stimulated the sales of "miracle" furniture polishes. Think about the messages given by thousands of TV furniture polish commercials: "fast and easy"; "polished clean and lint-free"; "see yourself reflected"; "Brand X shines your dingy furniture better than Grandma's beeswax and turpentine and it smells woody, lemony, and expensive."

Furniture care isn't that simple. There *are* some ways to cut the time spent caring for furniture and make it last longer. Notice I said "ways," not "way." It isn't done with a squirt of magic aerosol furniture polish as a TV or magazine ad might suggest.

My approach to furniture cleaning is more preventive than maintenance-oriented. Buy high-quality furniture—well-manufactured furniture, though it may be expensive to buy, costs less in the long run. Cheap furniture loses its crisp, elegant look rapidly and becomes conspicuously dull and shabby-looking. Once in this decrepit condition, it takes a lot of time and supplies to maintain it. And it rarely looks any better cleaned and polished than it did before you started. Select carefully and get good quality. Paying a little more cash will save a lot of your most precious commodity, personal time.

Choosing furniture with an eye to cleanability

The design and style of furniture you choose will determine how many hours per day, week, or year you will have to give to maintaining it. Elaborate grooves and carvings and decorations are going to take more time to keep looking good. And the more kinds of material furniture is made of (or a room is decorated with), the more time and types of equipment and supplies it will take to clean.

You are the sole judge on this one.

Which chair leg would you rather clean?

If the prestige or decor of your home calls for the elaborate unit, you have to decide the long-range value of owning it. No matter what you have in mind, check the furniture and make sure all the surfaces *can* be maintained. The wood should have a finish—not just an oiled surface or a colored stain, but a transparent varnish-type coat, called a "membrane finish," to prevent dirt and cleaning materials from penetrating into the wood. Lighter wood furniture shows less dust, is easier to make look good, and remains that way longer than darker furniture. Natural or bare wood that needs constant "feeding" or oiling is a pain to maintain and will look dull and discolored before long.

Metal should have a smooth finish, not be pitted or engraved. It should have a baked enamel or other hard-surfaced coating. Stainless steel and chrome are durable, but require a lot of effort to keep clean and bright.

Glass used as an overlay on a desk or table looks good and doesn't show dust, fingerprints, etc., too badly. But clear glass see-through units—coffee tables, end tables, breakfast tables—act like a magnifying glass. *Everything* shows—a piece of lint will look like a caterpillar carcass.

Is it cleanable?

Fabric will generally be the most used and abused part of furniture. Spillage on furniture is as common as on carpet, believe it or not. Some fabrics look superb, but stains and marks on them may never be removed. Ditto with cane and wicker furniture. But if you have your heart set on it, spray-enamel or spray-polyurethane cane and wicker the minute you have it inside the door; this will make it somewhat cleanable (depending on what you spill on it).

Scotchgard, which you can buy at the supermarket or hardware store and apply, is a lifesaver for most upholstery and for you personally. It is an excellent protection for most fabrics, making them more maintainable, because the fibers are protected. But if a big bowl of borscht gets upended and sends a tidal wave of red over the table and onto a Scotchgarded seat, you'll probably need to consult the spot and stain removal chart (pages 99-104).

Is it restorable?

Some fabrics look great when new, or newly cleaned, but after a few people sit on them, they become matted or shiny. You've all seen velvet or fur-type material after it has been sat on: A rump print remains, and you have better things to do than go around brushing up cushions to make them look good. Pick a fabric that "restores," or comes back to life, after use (or that doesn't need to "restore"). Select a hard-finish fabric for dining room chairs that are used constantly. White or light-colored fabrics (especially solid colors) show and accent every spot. Fabrics with some color blend or a pattern hide dirt better. Again, this is a matter of taste—but try to make it easy on yourself. Remember, furniture exists for your use and comfort.

Keeping furniture looking nice

Convinced that the secret of furniture maintenance is in the bottle or can of polish, the majority of us use

too much of it. We build up layers of gunk, which result in more work and sometimes even surface deterioration. A treated cloth that leaves no oil or residue, yet picks up dust, is the best way to go. Throw away your feather dusters (alias: dust spreaders). They are the least effective duster going. You can purchase treated paper dustcloths at your local janitorial supply house. They're called Masslinn cloths, and will last and last; when they're dirt-saturated you can throw them away. For quick light dusting and cobweb removal, those lovely lambswool (cotton-candy looking) dusters on a stick are amazing.

The pro approach might give you new ideas about furniture cleaning. My company cleans thousands of desktops, tabletops, chairs, stands, racks, and cabinets every night throughout the U.S. In most of our cleaning, we wipe with treated Masslinn cloths to remove dust. When fingermarks have to be removed, we use a light spray of neutral cleaner solution or a water-damp cloth to wipe, then dry-buff to a natural sheen. We avoid using polish where the finish can maintain its own luster.

If you use an aerosol polish, use it seldom and lightly. Select one type of polish and use it consistently. The reason for this is simple. Often your furniture surfaces will come out dull and streaked because your new polish isn't compatible with the old polish.

Select your polish on these merits:

1. *Ease of application*

2. *Lastingness of protection*

3. *Non-smearing and -streaking*

4. *Safety (you want a polish that's safe for your furniture surfaces—and for you to work with)*

5. *Pleasing scent*

6. *Easy buffing*

7. *Ability to hide superficial scratches and blemishes*

Types of polish

● *Clear oil treatment*

Usually a mineral oil, vegetable oil, turpentine blend, used to "feed" bare wood. Has high gloss when applied but it soon becomes a greasy film that collects dust and fingerprints.

● *Liquid or paste solvent*

Hard to apply. Excellent water and abrasion resistance. Low gloss, but durable.

● *Oil emulsion polish*

Cream type. Good cleaning properties but same drawbacks as clear oil.

● *Water or oil wax emulsion (aerosol or spray)*

Contains all components needed in a good polish: protects, enhances the beauty, makes it easy to dust. These are the buildup babies referred to a couple of pages back. Used once a year or so, they *are* good, but if you use them every time you clean they'll lay a thick layer of gunk on your pretty wood.

If you have raw or natural wood surfaces in your home, they'll need to be "fed," or treated to keep them from drying out and cracking. Lemon oil and other such treatments should be rubbed on. Take your time so the wood can absorb it, then wipe off the excess.

However, I think feeding wood is a ridiculous waste of effort and material. Besides, if grease or ink get on bare wood, it's ruined. Either low-gloss or satin-sheen finishes are available that seal the surface, forming a glass-like membrane through which that beautiful grain will still be bright and clear and fully visible. Marks and stains will end up on *it* instead of on the wood.

If you wish to apply (or reapply) a varnish or polyurethane membrane coat to ailing wood surfaces, it's easy. First, clean the surface with a strong cleaning solution—a strong ammonia solution, wax stripper, or degreaser if it's been sealed; solvent if raw—to take off all dirt and oils. Let it dry until any swollen grain goes down. Take care of any nicks or raised spots with a few strokes of superfine sandpaper, then wipe with a tack cloth or a cloth very lightly dampened with paint thinner to pick up any dust or lint on the surface. Finally, apply the varnish or polyurethane, paying attention to the directions on the container. It may take two coats.

Dusting

One of the simplest ways to keep your furniture looking nice is to keep it dusted. The frequency with which you need to dust depends on how dusty or polluted your area is, how readily your furniture shows dust, and how finicky you are.

Dust causes more mental anxiety to you than it does physical damage to your dwelling, so don't get your duster feathers ruffled. Dust is visually offensive and may strain your emotions when visitors drop by, but it does little harm unless someone in the family has an allergy. (Dust on floors and carpets *does* cause deterioration.) If I had a place I had to dust more than weekly, I'd move!

You can reduce dusting to a minor duty if:

1. *You place and maintain proper matting.*

2. *Your vacuum is working well and you use it. Empty your vacuum bag frequently, because if you vacuum when it's full you'll* create dust.*

3. *Your furnace and/or air conditioner filters are serviced regularly.*

4. *Your home is weatherproofed (door and window seals, caulking, etc.); weatherproofing keeps dust out, too.*

When you dust, don't use clouds of aerosol polish or puddles of oily wood treatments, because after a while, you'll create a waxy buildup that will not only look bad and be sticky and more difficult to clean, but actually attract and hold dust. Dust high places first. This gets the dead flies and other crud off the ledges onto the floor, where it can be vacuumed from easily. Always dust *before* you vacuum so that the crumbs and ashes and orange seeds in the corners and crannies of the furniture won't end up on a neatly vacuumed floor.

Use the right dusting tool. *Don't* use a feather duster. The air movement a feather duster causes will blow particles all over and you'll chase dust for hours. Instead, use one or more of these tools:

1. A water-dampened soft terry cleaning cloth (see Equipment Chart). Make sure it's thoroughly wrung out so it's only slightly damp. Terry dusters are easy to find or make and use. They won't damage surfaces or create extra work; they're excellent for removing and holding dust and other residue. Make sure, when you dust, to use all the surfaces of the cloth, rotating it often so it won't become a dust distributor. When it's dust-saturated, use another cloth. On glossy surfaces, buff behind the damp cloth with a dry cloth.

2. A Masslin cloth. This is a disposable chemically treated cloth with a "dry oil" in the fibers. It absorbs and picks up dust and small particles and is excellent for fine furniture. It will snag on rough surfaces (but any surface that rough should be vacuumed). When a cloth becomes saturated with dust (after about three months of daily use in the average-sized dwelling), simply pitch it and use a new one. These cloths leave a nice luster on wood and other finishes and cost only pennies. They're available at janitorial supply stores.

3. A lambswool duster. This is a fluffy ball of (sometimes synthetic) wool on the end of a 30-inch (or longer) stick. It looks like cotton candy on a stick, but almost magically picks up dust and particles and is especially good for high places, cobwebs, and Venetian or mini blinds. Shake it outside after use, vacuum it when it gets dust-saturated—and use it until it disintegrates. Lambswool dusters can be bought at a janitorial supply house or a local domestic store.

Cleaning fabric upholstery

As part of your routine cleaning, you should keep both vinyl and fabric upholstery vacuumed. You can use your upright on the seats of couches and chairs as you vacuum the carpet, or go over the whole piece with the upholstery attachment of your wet-dry. Slight surface dirt or hair and skin oils on fabric or vinyl can be removed with a cloth dampened in a carpet shampoo solution. Then wipe with a damp rinse cloth and rub dry with a towel. This kind of surface removal works well if you don't let the arms and seat get too dirty.

When upholstery really gets dirty, you probably ought to call a professional if you want to clean it right. But it *is* possible to do it yourself. If the fabric is thoroughly soiled, it should be washed with an upholstery cleaning solution or shampoo, then rinsed out. This is where problems arise in a do-it-yourself upholstery cleaning job. Cleaning solution is scrubbed on the dirt and the upholstery fabric seems to be cleaner. Actually, the surface dirt has been loosened and has sunk deeper into the fabric along with the cleaning solution. The fabric appears clean, but it isn't. The fabric is soaked with chemical, which leaves it sticky and matted down. The dirt and moisture have to be removed with an upholstery extractor attachment or a good wet-dry vacuum. Soon after the cleaning application, rinse with clear water and use the extractor again. But be sure to use water sparingly—don't get the backing or filling material wet!

To remove stains on clean upholstery, apply the same principles you do with carpet (see Chapter 10). A surface spot can be wiped or cleaned with an applicator dampened with cleaning solution and dried with a dry, absorbent cloth. Spotting kits with professional instructions are available from most large carpet distributors or a janitorial supply house.

Always be sure to check manufacturers' cleaning instructions.

Appliances

As in any cleaning, one of the most important principles in cleaning appliances is to keep them up: If you let your oven or refrigerator go three years between cleanings, of course it's going to be a depressing and time-consuming chore.

The basic rules of appliance cleaning are: Don't use abrasive scouring cleanser, metal scrapers, or harsh steel wool or abrasive (colored) nylon scouring pads on your appliances; these are damaging to enamel, stainless steel, and plastic surfaces alike. *Do* use a solution of heavy-duty cleaner or grease cutter in a spray bottle, a soft white (non-abrasive) nylon cleaning pad, and a drying towel to remove scum. If dirt and grease turn out to be stubborn, let the cleaning solution sit awhile to soften it. If you want an appliance exterior to really shine, use an alcohol-based evaporating window cleaner to polish it. To clean under and behind appliances, just use a radiator brush— but be sure to unplug *any* appliance before you start poking around in back of it (then you'll be sure to live to enjoy how clean it is!). Now for the particulars:

Stoves

Spend more time soaking and you'll spend less time scrubbing. Take the burner pans out, if you can, and dump them in hot, soapy water while you clean the rest of the unit. (If you really need to, you can use a tough green scrubbing sponge on the pans to remove the softened baked-on crud.) To clean the top, back, and sides of the stove, use a curly stainless metal "chore girl" type cleaning pad soaked with cleaning solution; The edges will pick up little bumps of hard grease but won't hurt the enamel or stainless steel surface. Rinse the pad well in hot water or the greasy lumps will harden in it.

Ovens

We all clean ovens the same way, and it's always a tough job. Apply oven cleaner, and wait, and wait some more. This is the most important step; the chemicals need time to loosen and dissolve all those drips and spatters and stone-hard lumps. When you've tested for the fourth time and the stuff finally seems to be coming off, wipe off the cleaner with heavy towels, using a green nylon or "chore girl" pad on

remaining crusty areas (such as near the elements). Be sure to wear rubber gloves and make sure there's plenty of ventilation. Oven cleaner is nasty stuff (for nasty work).

Refrigerators and freezers

Unplug the unit; empty it. In a bucket, mix a solution of three ounces of ammonia or disinfectant cleaner to three gallons of water. Using a soft white nylon cleaning sponge, wash the interior, sponging off hardened food, then buff with an absorbent cloth.

Stove hoods and exhaust vents

They can cause fires if they get too grease-laden, so don't neglect them. Besides, they're quick and simple to clean. Be sure to check the manufacturer's instructions, if any. Generally, you take off the grille, filter, or whatever and unplug the unit if you can. Clean off the sticky fuzzy grease with paper towels and a spray degreaser, being careful not to wet anything electrical or to spray anything into the motor. Non-mechanical parts, such as the grille, can soak in hot, soapy water for a while. Dry everything thoroughly, replace or clean any filters there may be, and reassemble.

12.

Shorter visits to the bath-room

The restroom in the commercial building was a sight to behold. A line of sinks stretched to infinity, and the toilet stalls looked like the starting gate at Santa Anita. This huge restroom was used by 250 people, and it just radiated cleanliness. The chrome glistened, and the porcelain of the sinks and toilets sparkled germ-free. All toilet paper and handtowel dispensers were filled. And the matron only spent an hour per day to keep it that way.

Clean your bathroom in 3 1/2 minutes

Considering the average home bathroom's size and use, and that matron's production time, you should be able to keep your bathroom in that same immaculate condition in 3½ minutes a day! Sound impossible? Not if you put some professional techniques to work. The "commercial approach" to cleaning your bathroom is simple and will save you time—the secret, of course, being to spend a few minutes each day keeping it clean rather than indulge in a big once-a-week clean-and-scrub siege. The preventive approach here—maintaining your bathroom regularly and efficiently—is smart.

Tools and supplies again are important. You'll have to bite your lip and disregard most of the old standbys like abrasive cleansers, acid bowl cleaners, deodorant sprays, magic toilet spices, perfumed blocks, wonder wicks, and blue bowl seltzers.

Essential supplies

For periodic removal of hard water or mineral buildup, the old cleanser—or mild phosphoric acid—has its use, even by the professional. The best procedure to follow, however, is a regular cleaning program that eliminates the need for these.

To avoid wasted time, damage to fixtures, and poor results, you should go to the local janitorial supply house and purchase scented or unscented disinfectant cleaner concentrate—it's what hospitals use. (Be sure to get a *quaternary* cleaner; its active ingredient is ammonium chloride. Avoid the phenol-based cleaners; they're too toxic for home use.) This liquid, if diluted according to the directions on the bottle and used correctly, will clean quickly and efficiently, and eradicate or retard bacterial growth. This will eliminate not only smells but the need for the expensive perfumed preparations you've been using. While at the janitorial supply house, pick up one plastic spray bottle for each bathroom so the bottle can be left in the room.

Once the spray bottle is filled with the water and disinfectant cleaner in the correct proportion, the only other tools you need are a cleaning cloth and a two-sided scouring sponge of cellulose and white nylon mesh (for dislodging any persistent residue).

Your daily bathroom cleaning routine should be something like this: Spray and wipe the mirror if it's spotted. If not, leave it alone. Next, spray the hardware, sink, and countertops (spray ahead so the

For daily bathroom maintenance

Use germicidal or disinfectant cleaner diluted from concentrate.

Dilute according to directions into a plastic spray bottle.

Spray the mirror, fixtures, sink, and countertops. Wipe and buff dry. Next do the shower stall and tub. Then the toilet (base last!) and floor. Remember that odors are caused by bacteria. A clean bathroom won't need deodorant.

cleaner will soften and break down soil); wipe and buff the surfaces dry. They will sparkle. Do shower stalls and tubs next. Do the toilet stool last. (See pages 116-117.)

Once the upper fixtures are clean, fall to your knees (one minute won't hurt you). Spray the floor, and with the already damp cleaning cloth, wipe it up. This method is a lot faster and better than mixing up mop water and fumbling around with a mop in a 15- to 20-square-foot area.

The benefits of preventive maintenance

It takes only minutes to clean a bathroom the spray-disinfectant way, and if you leave a spray bottle and cloth in the room, you can get your bathroom spotless while you're waiting for Junior to go potty or for the sink to fill up. The system works only if you clean the bathroom regularly, however. This keeps hard water deposits, soap scum, toilet bowl lines, and other soils from building up and cementing on. The basic reason you needed abrasive cleansers and acids (and dynamite) to clean the bathroom in the past was that buildup accumulated to the point of no return and had to be ground off instead of wiped off.

Don't use powdered cleansers and steel wool to grind dirt off surfaces. In most of the many hundreds of houses I've cleaned in my career, the sinks, tubs, and shower units—porcelain or plastic—have had damage from improper use of acids, cleansers, and abrasive pads. The grinding abrasion that removes spots and stains also removes chrome and porcelain. This is a great reason to use the disinfectant cleaner/spray bottle system from the start. Your chrome, plastic, fiberglass, marble, and porcelain will remain bright and sound.

If you have damaged fixtures, you'll have difficulty no matter what you use because porous surfaces collect gunk fast and clean slow. Many of these surfaces—especially the shower area—will benefit from a coat of paste wax, which helps repel the scum and hard water buildup. After attending my seminar, many a housekeeper minimizes the problem of shower buildup by simply hanging a 10- or 12-inch squeegee in the shower. It takes only fifteen seconds for the user to leave the wall dry and clean after a shower. (Besides, squeegeeing in the nude is a unique experience!) But if you let hard water dry on your faucets and shower walls over and over again, the built-up minerals practically need to be chiseled off.

Be careful with those things the hint and tip books tell you to soak in tubs and sinks overnight (like oven grills, blinds, crusted camping gear, tools, etc.). Extended exposure to some normally harmless cleaners will often pit the fixtures.

Keep your drains running free by pulling out the stopper every month or so and cleaning the collected hair off it (encouraging hair care to be practiced elsewhere than over the sink can prevent this). Boiling hot water poured down a drain periodically ought to handle any soap scum buildup that might slow drainage down.

When a drop of hard or soapy water lands on a surface and dries, the minerals and other residue dissolved in it collect at the base of the drop when it evaporates. Every time the surface gets wet, new drops add to the accumulation—and this will keep building up into a hard, solid deposit. That's why it's smart to clean regularly (especially showers and windows) and not give buildup a chance to happen.

It's fast and easy to clean up when fresh but like cement if you wait!

Cleaning toilets

Briskly scrubbing inside a toilet bowl with a bowl brush for a few seconds each day will retard buildup and remove discoloration and lines. When you do your daily spray-cleaning of the bathroom with disinfectant cleaner, spray and wipe the entire outside of the toilet from top to bottom. Contrary to popular belief, it's the outside of the toilet that's most unsanitary. Be sure to do the base of the toilet last. This will prevent you from transporting the worst germ concentration to the faucet handles. Every couple of weeks, pour a little disinfectant into the bowl, swish the water around, and let it sit awhile. Remember, it's the *outside* of the toilet—under the seat and around the

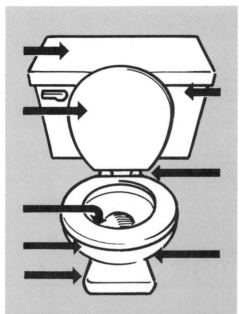

Be sure to clean all surfaces. And work your way from the top to the floor.

Basic bowl cleaner technique

For daily maintenance, scrub briskly inside the bowl with a bowl brush. You only need to use acid bowl cleaner a couple of times a year. When you do . . .

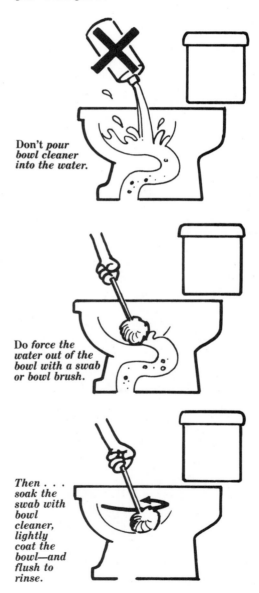

Don't *pour bowl cleaner into the water.*

Do *force the water out of the bowl with a swab or bowl brush.*

Then . . . *soak the swab with bowl cleaner, lightly coat the bowl—and flush to rinse.*

rim—that's germiest and will begin to smell if not cleaned frequently. The cold water that enters the bowl with every flush discourages bacterial growth there.

If you need to remove old buildup in the toilet, do it right. Don't pour steaming acid into the water-filled bowl and slosh it around. Dilution with water neutralizes the power of any bowl cleaner. Instead, a couple of times a year, grasp a swab (see Equipment Chart) and push it quickly up and down in the bowl toward the "throat" of the toilet. All the water will "vanish" (no free advertising intended). Then give the swab a light application of bowl cleaner and coat the inside of the toilet bowl. Flush to rinse.

If a ring remains, don't get excited and acid-bath the whole unit. The ring is the result of hard water deposit that's left as water in the toilet evaporates. A pumice stone will remove almost any ring (be sure the surface is wet or it will scratch).

Remember to brush the bowl regularly to prevent buildup. And bear in mind that bleach is not a good cleaning compound: It is an aggressive oxidizing agent. It appears to clean things, but this appearance is often deceptive. The oxidizing (whitening) of stains, toilet rings, rust stains, etc., generally doesn't remove them, only bleaches or camouflages them. Bleach will eventually break down chrome and Formica and other plastic laminates. Keep it out of your bathrooms!

Toilet-tank capsules that turn the water blue don't do much for maintaining toilets, since many of them are only colored bleaching agents. Their greatest value is psychological. If you practice good cleaning habits in the bathroom, you won't need them.

How to get rid of bathroom mildew

When warm, humid weather and spores of mold team up, those little black spots of mildew can grow on everything, including drawers, closets, books, and shoes. But, aside from the basement, mildew's favorite home is the bathroom.

For the first twenty years of my life, I thought mildew was something that only appeared on roses and alfalfa. Since entering the cleaning business, I've been bombarded with the mildew question: "How do we get rid of it?" The best way to get rid of it is to prevent it. See Chapter 8 for household-wide tips for preventing mildew.

Using disinfectant in the bathroom and shower areas discourages its growth there. And chlorine bleach "kills" mildew, but won't prevent it from returning; you can only do that by altering conditions favorable for its growth. But drying out a bathroom that several people bathe and shower in every day is difficult, so all you can really do is keep cleaning with disinfectant—and hitting mildewed grout with a weak chlorine bleach solution, as long as the tile isn't made of plastic and you're careful not to get the bleach on anything that is.

Doorknobs, handbags, and telephones

If people were asked to list the most unsanitary objects in the home, most of them would remember the toilet, but forget doorknobs. It wouldn't hurt, while armed with a spray bottle of disinfectant cleaner, to go through the house and spray and wipe all the doorknobs occasionally. (And the light switches, chair backs, and telephone receivers.)

Another unsanitary item that all women should be aware of is the purse or handbag. Purses are often placed on dining tables (right next to the salad fork) after having been set on the floor alongside the toilet in a public restroom. Avoid this unappetizing practice! Set your purse by your chair—and use the purse shelves provided in public restrooms, when available.

13.

Success in high places

One of my customers had a husband full of ambition and desire to clean, but he was terrified of high places. She would hire me to wash all the high areas, saving the low stuff for him. One year while doing his low section, he was on a plank just a foot off the floor when he was seized by the phobia. He lay down on the plank, dug his whitened fingertips into the wood of the plank, and froze there. His wife, unable to talk him down from that dizzying height, ended up calling the fire department (siren and all!). They finally dislodged the husband's death grip on the plank and got him onto floor level safely, but he was never sound enough emotionally to assist in cleaning again.

Be sure to adjust or limit the reaching of tall areas to fit your resources, age, nerves (and your helpers' bravery!). But don't be buffaloed by hard-to-reach areas. "Once I got up there, it only took ten minutes" is the wail of many "end-of-the-day" housekeepers. The many hours spent to get going is the bane of cleaning in high places. Easy access contributes greatly to success in such cleaning, yet the shaky old ladder and unsteady step stool are about the extent of most homes' scaffolding.

More energy, time, and emotion are used going up and down the ladder or stool than actually doing the job at hand. And all of our effort, worry, tool procurement and arrangement seem to be focused on the few minutes we'll actually be performing the job, instead of trying to save the hours getting in position to start it.

As a professional housecleaner, I too have to weigh the same factors a homemaker does. The equipment needed to get at the work has to be light enough to be manageable, and small enough to fit in tight areas and keep from scratching walls and woodwork. It must be *sturdy* and *safe* enough to ensure no falls. The following equipment are the basics that thirty years of housecleaning have taught me to use.

A 5-foot ladder is just right for household cleaning

A good ladder

4-foot   6-foot   5-foot

A plain old common ladder is one of your best all-around tools. It's versatile, manageable, and safe . . . if you choose the right model. For household use, the perfect stepladder size is five feet high. Four-foot ladders are too short to work on 8-foot ceilings; a 6-foot ladder is too high, and it nicks up the house when you carry it around. A 5-foot ladder is just right for most household cleaning operations. Instead of buying several creaky wooden ladders for $20 each during your lifetime, buy a 5-foot heavy-duty commercial aluminum ladder for $35-$50. You'll never regret it. It's strong, safe to use anywhere, and will probably outlast you, even counting the ten years it may add to your life. It can be used outside on rough terrain and bad weather or dry storage won't hurt it.

For higher reaches every household should also have a tall ladder like the ones firefighters use, and I feel the perfect one for this purpose is an 18-foot, two-piece extension ladder. It will collapse to 10 feet for storage in the laundry room or inside the stairwell and lengthen out safely to 16 feet—enough to get the cat out of the tree, put up the aerial, or paint the trim every five years. Aluminum is lighter, but in an extension ladder for home use, I prefer wood or fiberglass for safety and electrical protection. Don't paint wooden ladders—paint hides breaks, cracks, and flaws and is slippery when wet. Instead, use boiled linseed oil to maintain wooden ladders. It penetrates the wood, keeps water out and slivers in. A coat every five years will keep a ladder happy.

Make yourself a box

To reach high cabinets, curtain rods, etc., people usually climb on the harmless-looking kitchen stool or bench. These have a narrow base and a deceptively sturdy top. But they're too unbalanced and risky to use as a standing or cleaning tool. To replace the old bench—and the equally unsafe chair, which has battered many a body—a simply constructed box of ¾-inch plywood is inexpensive and far superior. I'd suggest dimensions of 15x20x28 inches or smaller (see next page). The telephone companies have a similar unit they've used safely and effectively for years. It's called a "three-position stool." Laid flat on its side or end, it gives you three low heights to work from. Hand holes can be cut in the box's side to move it, and it can serve for storage when it's not in use. It can also serve as a baby crib, an extra chair when company comes, or to hide the puppy on Christmas Eve.

Just lay out the following plan and assemble per directions. If your husband has traded in his $300 power saw to buy you a new vacuum, no sweat—a $39.95 sabre saw will work fine!

Laid flat on its side or end, it gives you three low heights to work from. Hand holes can be cut in the box's side to move it. Use it for storage when it's not in use.

This simply constructed box is inexpensive and a far better way to reach the high places. I'd suggest dimensions of 15"x20"x28." You can make it larger or smaller to custom-fit you or your stepladder.

Materials needed:
1 4' x8' sheet of ¾" exterior plywood
1 pound of No. 8 finish nails
1 bottle of white glue
sandpaper
1 pint of clear varnish or polyurethane

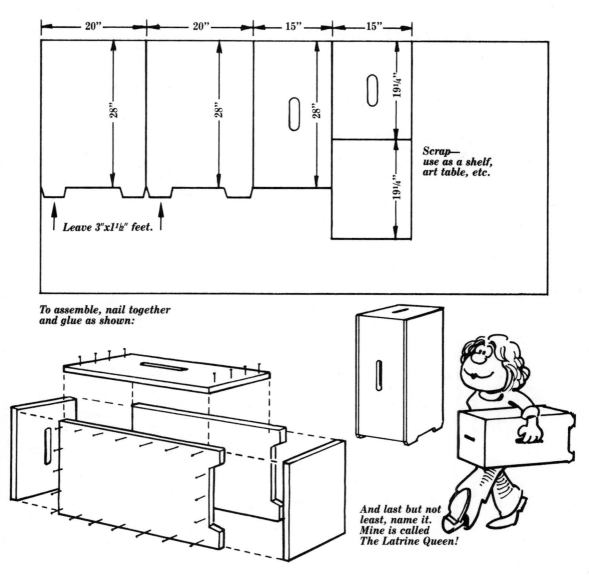

Scrap—
use as a shelf,
art table, etc.

Leave 3"x1½" feet.

To assemble, nail together and glue as shown:

And last but not least, name it. Mine is called The Latrine Queen!

Walk the plank for safety

The last and most useful tool to help you conquer the unreachable places is a sturdy, ordinary 2x12-inch plank eight to ten feet long. Purchase it at a lumberyard and make sure it has no loose knots, cracks, or weak areas. Redwood is good because it's light and rot-resistant. (Pine and hemlock will also work all right, but they're not nearly as light.) Sand off the corners and rough edges for ease of handling, and it's ready to use. Don't paint or varnish it or it will be slippery when wet. You'll use the plank for many things. It is one of the best "under-$20" investments you'll ever make. The idea is to combine the stepladder, extension ladder, box, and plank in a number of ways to reach your working area easily, safely, and without wasted motion. If you need to reach higher areas than can be reached with this combination, you should rent the necessary equipment, because

you'll seldom use it around the house.

A plank, though it may be scary to you at first, is safe to work on if you're reasonably awake. You'll soon get used to the slight spongy "give" you'll feel on the plank. Planks were only fatal to blindfolded pirates when they had to walk off the end. Looking up at the ceiling and moving toward the box end of the plank puts you in the same circumstance as the pirates. That's why you should always keep an extra sponge or empty bucket at the end of the plank so a nudge of the toe reminds you to stop walking. (This is a case where "kicking the bucket" is an aid to longevity.) The plank-and-ladder combination is especially effective to use in high stairwells. On stair landings and other open areas, you can figure out a combination (such as the one above). It will make you love yourself for your brilliance.

Most of the time, doing ceilings in a house from a ladder, you're only two feet off the floor. When in a stairwell, you are higher over the stairs, but with the walls of the narrow landing on

For maximum stability, be sure your plank extends a few inches beyond the end of the box and beyond the ladder rung it's set on.

124

To clean a stair landing—

Lean your extension ladder (padded with a towel or dry sponges) against the wall with the base angled into the stairs. Open your stepladder at the top of the stairs. The plank, set across a lower rung of the stepladder and a rung of the extension ladder, puts you in a safe, convenient position to clean or paint the walls. Padding the "wall" end of your plank if it touches the wall will protect the wall.

both sides of you and with a ladder at both ends, there is little risk of falls. I've seen twenty ladder accidents for every plank-and-ladder accident.

Regular or extension ladders must be tilted at the proper angle to keep them from slipping down or tumbling over. One foot out from the base of the wall for every four feet up is just right. Keep your cleaning solution, tools, paint, and other working materials as close to you as possible by wearing a pocketed apron or setting your gear on the plank. Ascending or descending a ladder or plank for every dip depletes strength, wastes time, and exposes you more often to mishap.

One "trick" I've tried without much success is moving a folding stepladder without moving the buckets or tools. I bat about 60 percent. The other 40 percent has cost me wet carpets, skinned shins, painted faces, and starting over again. It is also

extremely risky to tie or lay a plank on planters, metal railings, fireplace mantels, or other trim. Most of these were designed to be looked at, not to support 150 pounds or more of plank, cleaning tools, and person. Mortar is not stout. It spaces rocks and bricks for compressed strength, but not tensile strength. Place ladders and planks on supports where strength is certain.

A cleaning towel (see Chapter 14) slipped over each of the ladder's upper legs will keep it from marking up your walls. A dry sponge (Chapter 14) under each leg will prevent it from slipping if the surface the legs rest on is questionable. Tennis shoes on *your* feet will prevent *you* from slipping, too.

A final word of advice: Put your name on your ladders and planks. When your neighbors spot them, they will be only too happy to try out your new way of reaching high places.

To use a ladder safely: Angle 1 foot from the wall for every 4 feet of height. Never stand on the top rung.

Be sure to adjust or limit the reaching of high areas to fit your age, nerves, and bravery. If you have an overwhelming fear of heights, don't do it . . . you'll get hurt. If you have no fear of heights, get smart . . . you *can* get hurt! If heights make you shake in your boots, find a couple of daredevils and bake them some cookies. Let *them* climb to clean off that flyspeck, change a light bulb, paint, or wash the ceiling.

14.

I once bid to wash walls in six large offices, a long hall, lobby, entrances, and storage areas in a Massey-Ferguson tractor dealer's office. Back in the '60s when a dollar was a dollar, I was the low bid at the price of $275. Our new crew was busy on the scheduled day, so I tackled the job alone. Seven hours later, I had it finished and more than a few compliments on the quality of the job. On another occasion, I washed all the walls, ceilings, and woodwork in a modern three-bedroom home in less than one day—alone. Now, I'm no more a "super" wall and ceiling cleaner than you are. In fact, I'm certain that many of you could keep up with or beat me on my best day, if you'd use the same approach I did.

There are two reasons why wall and ceiling cleaning will become one of

Simplified wall & ceiling cleaning

your favorite housecleaning tasks when you do it my way: (1) It's easy and trouble-free and (2) the delight of seeing the surface come clean is great! In fact, you're going to find washing your walls and ceilings so easy and satisfying, you'll want to wash your friends' walls and ceilings just to show off. Your days of struggling with a bucket of grimy wall-washing solution will end as you finish this chapter, if you follow the simple principles it sets forth.

We outlined the basic principle of cleaning—eliminate, saturate, dissolve, remove— in Chapter 6; here's how that principle applies to the technique and tools of wall cleaning. Your height, your arm strength, and the degree of dirt accumulated doesn't make much difference in the time and effort it

takes to clean walls and ceilings. Using your head and the right tools *will* make a difference.

The versatile dry sponge

One of the first and most important (and least known) tools of housecleaning is a rubber sponge, sometimes chemically treated, called a dry sponge. The dry sponge works just like a rubber eraser, removing and absorbing dirt. Dry sponges are generally tan or red in color and come on handles, or as flat 7x6x½-inch pads. The pad is by far the better way to go because it has a larger number of usable surfaces.

Dry sponges are great for cleaning wallpaper, oil paintings, and smoke or soot damage. Dry sponges also work well on acoustical tile ceilings, masonry surfaces, and most flat-painted walls and ceilings.

The proper way to hold a dry sponge is illustrated here, to utilize each pad's eight surfaces.

Dry sponges come wrapped in cellophane to keep the chemical they're impregnated with fresh. When you unwrap them, they feel dry and spongy. Never, never use water on them or get them wet (not a drop)—or they will become useless for cleaning. Most people use dry sponges for cleaning wallpaper. (Now more of you will know what I'm referring to.) They are excellent on wallpaper—much better than "dough" wallpaper cleaners that crumble and stick!

On ceiling acoustical tile and on most flat oil- or latex-painted walls, one swipe of a dry sponge will remove the dirt. It won't remove fingerprints or flyspecks or grease—only the film of dirt. In most homes, dry-sponging the ceiling will leave it perfect. I've washed behind a dry sponge many times, not believing that the sponge could get all the dirt out, but it did— every bit of it! In fact, on many porous walls or painted surfaces, even where the dirt is embedded deeply, a dry sponge is superior to washing. Even on walls that are smoke-damaged, ten minutes of dry-sponging the room prior to washing will reduce washing time

and expense more than 50 percent. When dry-sponging, you don't have to stop to dip or rinse. Just get to the surface and swipe in four-foot lengths (or shorter if your arms are shorter). The sponge will absorb the dirt and begin to get black. It will hold the dirt as you clean along, but as soon as its saturation point is reached you must turn and/or refold the sponge and keep going. The residue that falls from the sponge won't stain or stick, and is easily vacuumed up after the job is done.

Each pad-type sponge has eight good surfaces, if used correctly. (The handled dry sponges are great, except that once their single cleaning surface is saturated, the sponge is no longer usable.) When a dry sponge is black on both sides, throw it away. Washing them doesn't work. Dry sponges cost about a dollar and a half and are worth ten times that for the job they do and the time they save.

A dry sponge won't clean enamel or greasy surfaces, so don't be disappointed when you make a swipe across the kitchen or bathroom wall and nothing dramatic happens.

If you go into the bedroom and make a swipe across the ceiling or outside wall and can't see where you've just been, they don't need cleaning and the rest of the room probably doesn't either. Just clean the light fixtures and the woodwork and take off the rest of the hour you allowed for bedroom cleaning.

Once the dry-sponging is out of the way, the remaining areas, not cleaned with a dry sponge, will have to be washed. This can be accomplished rather simply if the right tools and methods are used.

Your rag is your worst enemy

There is no question that the most famous household cleaning tool is the simple little item known as a "rag." Your rags have been salvaged from ancient sheets, tattered diapers, worn-out T-shirts, feed sacks, and other fabric scraps. Using a rag to clean with

is like using a rake to comb your hair: ineffective. For 500 years cloth manufacturers have been working to develop fabrics that repel liquids and stains. They've succeeded, and we have scores of fabrics today that resist moisture—which makes them terrible cleaning tools. Yet we can't seem to resist saving trouser legs, old tricot slips, and a thousand other unsuitable fabrics for cleaning rags. Don't do it!

I'm certain that one thing that makes the professional a three times faster—and better—cleaner than the homemaker is the fact that homemakers are hung up on rags. Rags are only good for paint cleanup, stuffing rag dolls, blowing your nose, attracting antelopes in the Wyoming desert, or signaling surrender when the cleaning gets you down. Henceforth, the term "rag" must be banished from your housecleaning vocabulary and from your basket of cleaning tools. The rag in your housecleaning tool bag will be replaced with an item called a "cleaning cloth."

The noble cleaning cloth

A cleaning cloth is made from a new or salvaged heavy Turkish (cotton terrycloth) towel. I've had a lot of questions as to what kind of toweling to use. The big worry is that the new poly/cotton blends aren't as absorbent as the old pure cotton towels. Not so! They're an improvement! The polyester is used for the base fabric and the cotton to make the pile (nap). Moisture rarely gets to the base anyway, and the polyester dries faster and resists wrinkles. (A wrinkle-resistant cleaning cloth—now *that's* class!) But do be sure to use toweling with a high cotton content.

First cut the towel into an 18x18-inch flat piece, then fold it over and sew the one long side, leaving it open on both ends like a tube. (Be sure to hem the edge.) By folding the tube twice, you have a hand-sized surface of thick absorbent terrycloth that will efficiently cover every inch of surface it passes over—even get down into bumpy-textured walls and floors. It's not like the old linen bedsheet that just streaks and smears the film around. (We wouldn't think of drying *ourselves* on a piece of sheet after a bath.)

If you refold your cleaning towels right and use both sides, you have eight efficient surfaces to use; turn the towel inside out and you have eight

How to make a cleaning cloth

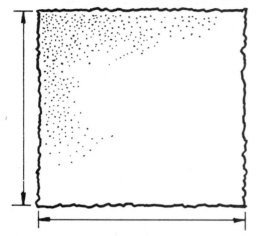

Cut an 18"x18" square of heavy terrycloth.

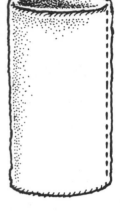

Fold and stitch together on the long side; hem the edges.

It will be hollow like a tube.

How to use it

Fold once—

then again—

& it will just fit your hand.

Soiled cleaning cloths are simply washed and tumble-dried for reuse.

By changing sides, and turning it inside out, you have 16 sides to clean with.

more. Sixteen surfaces on one little cleaning cloth! (Terry cleaning cloths are great to protect the hands from scrapes, cuts, and ripped fingernails, too.) I often clean all the walls of a large room using only three cleaning cloths. When you're finished and the cleaning cloths are damp and dirty, throw them in the washer.

You don't have to use much detergent, because the towels will be full of the cleaner you've been using. If you wash the towels while they're still wet, they'll come out as clean as they were before you used them (although in time they'll get dingy and battle-scarred; they'll still be clean, just stained). Don't hang them on the line or they will be stiff as a board and impossible to use the next time: Be sure to tumble-dry them! Twenty cleaning cloths will clean your entire house and, if washed properly, will last for years.

Your basic wall cleaning tools

The dry sponge and cleaning cloth are the main "professional" tools you need to do your wall cleaning, so don't prepare yourself a long list of materials and equipment. The rest of the items you probably already have around the house, so round them up: one empty bucket (plastic won't skin up the furniture or sweat like metal does), one bucket half full of warm water, an ordinary cellulose sponge (preferably about 1½ inches thick; make sure the other dimensions fit your hand), and some all-purpose neutral cleaner (I always add a little ammonia to cut grease—besides, I like to see my hands shrivel up!). That's it!

(I know what you're thinking now. "Man, wouldn't a two-compartment bucket be great!" No . . . it wouldn't. They are, without question, one of the most worthless instruments ever palmed off on a housecleaner. Just try to pour dirty water out of one side and keep clean water in the other—or carry the thing!)

Mix your cleaning solution following directions on the container. Make sure your cleaning compound is one capable of cutting the dirt you want to remove. Ammonia or good commercial neutral cleaner concentrates will be fine unless you're dealing with an extremely grease-laden kitchen, where a little ammoniated wax stripper or degreaser added to the solution will make the job much easier. For bathroom walls, you might want to use a disinfectant cleaner.

Before beginning, reinforce your attitude. I've read books and articles on cleaning house that say, "Allow yourself a day to a week for each room." You're going to clean it, not rebuild it! If you hustle, you should be able to wash a room in thirty minutes, but you'll probably want to allow yourself an hour (maybe more if you anticipate being interrupted). Prolonging a simple job will wear down your initiative and determination.

Cleaning procedure

You have your ladder or scaffolding in position, and now you're ready to begin my method of wall cleaning. You won't have to cover everything because there will be little or no dripping. (If you have a grand piano that a drop might hurt, don't take the chance: Throw a dropcloth or sheet of light plastic over it.) Upholstered furniture can usually be moved out of the way rather than covered. A drop of cleaning solution won't hurt anything if it's removed immediately. If it's not, it may spot or ruin the finish.

Your solution should be where you don't have to climb thirty feet to dip your sponge. Placing your bucket of solution in the right place is extremely important. ALWAYS KEEP IT AS CLOSE TO YOUR WORKING AREA AS POSSIBLE. Spilling solution was a major problem in my beginning housecleaning days. I finally learned to set the bucket next to me near the wall—not in back of me, or on a table,

To clean a wall

a bucket half filled with a warm ammonia or neutral cleaner solution . . .

an empty bucket . . .

a sponge . . .

a cleaning cloth.

1.

Dip the sponge about ½ inch into the solution.

2.

Start at the top of the wall and spread the solution to dissolve the soil. Then go back over the wetted-down area with your sponge and wipe to remove the soil.

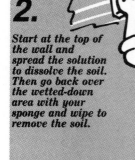

3.

Wipe the sponged area with a folded cleaning cloth.

4.

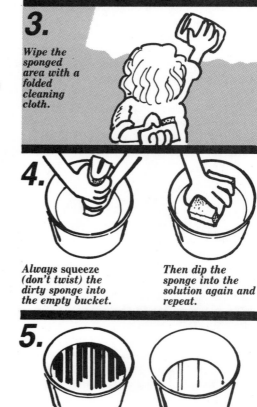

Always squeeze (don't twist) the dirty sponge into the empty bucket.

Then dip the sponge into the solution again and repeat.

5.

When you finish, the empty bucket will be full of dirty water.

Your cleaning solution will stay crystal clear—the chemical will always be working full strength for you.

132

or in the middle of the floor. Be sure to set it in a visible spot. The most common spillage problems are tripping over buckets or moving a piece of furniture behind which a full bucket of solution is hidden. If you do spill it on carpet, run for the wet-dry vacuum and get all the moisture out you can. Then rinse with clear water to get the ammonia (or other cleaning agent) out. Again, remember to fill your buckets only half full (if you fill them to the brim they'll be top-heavy and can easily spill), and keep the dirty bucket dumped in the toilet regularly (after each room), for if it spills you'll have a tough cleanup problem.

Take your sponge and dip it into the solution about ½ inch (not all the way in). This will give you plenty of solution to wet the wall or ceiling and leave the rest of the sponge dry enough to absorb any water that otherwise would splash into your eyes or run down your arms and down your back and into your shoes.

I know all the books say to start at the bottom of the wall and work up, because if you dribble on the lower unwashed wall from the top, it might stain: an old wives' tale. Anyone who tells you that doesn't know how to wash walls. In extreme cases with, say, 50-year-old paints or spectacularly dirty walls, it might be wise, but I think it's discouraging to start at the bottom, get it clean, then go on to the top and dribble on the clean wall. I can't stand to back up and redo an area I've already done. So I start at the top and recommend that you do the same.

How large an area you work on at one time depends, of course, on (1) your reach; (2) how soiled the surface is; and (3) how fast the solution will dry on the surface. A 3x3-foot section is just about right for the average person. Quickly cover the section with the solution on the sponge. Don't press hard or water will spurt out and drip on the carpet and your head. Gently spread the liquid on the surface. By the time you get to the end of the patch of wall you're working on, the initial application of solution has worked the dirt loose. Now go back to the starting point and again go over the area gently. Don't squeeze the sponge! By now, the dirt should be loosened by the chemicals in your cleaning solution and will come off and soak into the sponge. In the other hand, folded to perfection, is your cleaning cloth, with which you quickly wipe and buff the area before it dries. No rinsing is necessary. The wiping will not only remove the remaining cleaner and dirt, but will polish off the scum that so often streaks washed walls.

Now the critical procedure: Hold the sponge over the empty bucket and *squeeze*, don't wring (you only wring your hands or a chicken neck). When you squeeze the sponge, the dirty solution will go into the empty bucket, leaving the sponge damp and clean. Again dip the sponge ½ inch into the bucket of cleaning solution and repeat the process until the room is bright and clean.

You'll notice that the empty bucket is beginning to fill with filthy black gunk, while the cleaning solution is still crystal clear. The sponge you're dipping into the bucket of solution each time is a squeezed-out hungry sponge (not a sponge full of dirty cleaner), so the dirt never touches your cleaning solution. This means that every drop going on each new section of wall is powerful, unpolluted cleaning solution that will do most of the work. The old

Go easy on the solution. You'll be shocked what too much will do for you!

method you once used—scrubbing, dipping your sponge in the solution, wringing it, and scrubbing again— always left your cleaning water murky and filthy and thus without full cleaning power. It would streak the walls and have to be changed every fifteen minutes, taking up a lot of time and wasting a lot of cleaning solution. With the two-bucket method you don't spend time scrubbing, just applying and removing. And the towel dries and polishes walls three times as well as the old rags you once used.

"Outside walls" (the inside surfaces of exterior walls) will be dirtier than inside or "partition" walls, so don't be surprised. If you can't see where you're going when you wash, forget it—it doesn't need washing!

Two-bucket benefits

Besides doing a 70 percent faster and better job, the two-bucket wall cleaning technique has two more great "Life After Housework savers":

1. *You'll never dump and refill another bucket of solution. One bucket of water and 13¢ worth of solution will do all the walls in your house!*

2. *The dirty water . . . you will love it. In fact you will have a special relationship to it. Before, all your evidence of toil and accomplishment*

went down the drain; now you have it for show. I've seen people save it for days. (Bottle it and place it on the mantel.) I guarantee it will be the best, most heartwarming exhibit in your housekeeping museum.

Enameled walls

When cleaning enamel-painted halls, kitchen areas, or bathrooms, use the same procedure, with one simple adjustment: Keep the drying towels cleaner and drier, because enamel needs more polishing with a drier buffing cloth than flat paint. Wipe marks won't show on flat paints, but they will show even on perfectly clean enamel. Those circular wipe marks that you can't see when you finish (but can later on in certain light) are caused by rags; rags can't/won't buff-dry your walls. I was called back on many jobs during my first year of cleaning to remove streaks that weren't there when I left. Since that day twenty-five years ago when I began to use terry cleaning cloths I haven't been called back for a single case of "enamel streak."

What to do about wall spots

When you run into marks and spots on the walls that don't come clean when you wash them, just leave them until you finish. Then come back and try first to remove them by rubbing hard with a cleaning cloth and a little solution. Toothpaste, peanut butter, or abrasive cleansers will get them, but will also take off the paint or at least kill the sheen on the wall. Don't try to clean spots before you wash the whole wall down—they might come off with the first washing. LET THE SOLUTION DO THE WORK!

Most marks on walls can be removed by simply finding a cleaning agent with the same base as the spot. On a tar spot, for example, you can scrub and rub with high-powered cleaners, sweat and swear, and not get the spot; a little turpentine or paint thinner will remove it in three seconds and not hurt the wall. Use your head, not your hands—you won't scour the paint off or streak the surfaces.

How to clean :

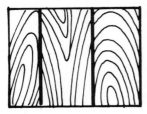

PANELING. Same procedure as for painted walls. Use neutral cleaner or organic oil soap solution, keeping the sponge nearly dry, and then, buffing with the grain, dry completely with a cleaning cloth.

VINYL WALLS. Use the cleaner recommended by the manufacturer, keeping the sponge nearly dry. Use no harsh or abrasive cleaners. Then dry thoroughly with a cleaning cloth.

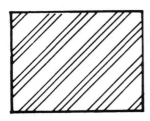

WALLPAPER. Use a dry sponge and clean with the flow of the design.

Cleaning woodwork

You can wash the woodwork or baseboards while doing the walls, but I seldom do, because woodwork is covered with lint, hair, dead gnats, etc., that will get into your sponge and be difficult to get out. Wait until you're finished washing the room and you have a damp cloth remaining from the wall washing. Wipe the baseboard, picking up all the residue, then use your sponge and a fresh cleaning towel to finish it up, if need be, streak- and lint-free.

How to clean paneling

Remember that raw wood must be coated with a finish so that moisture won't penetrate it. Then you'll be cleaning the finish, not the wood itself—it's faster, and much easier on the wood and you!

Don't be like the homemaker who decided to leave the wood paneling in her new home unfinished. She loved that natural wood look because of its homeyness and warm appearance. But then one afternoon, her children got into the Crisco and the crayons, and a generous percentage of the mess ended up on the wood wall. No matter how she scrubbed or what formula she tried, the spots and marks remained.

She should have finished the wood with low-luster varnish or polyurethane. This would have formed a protective shield on the surface of the wood that would keep grease and marks from penetrating into the wood and warping or staining it. A flat or satin resinous or polyurethane finish will dry with a low sheen and preserve the natural look of the wood. (Follow the instructions on the can, remember to stir well, and keep your work area as dust-free as you can.)

On wood paneling with a sealed surface, or vinyl paneling, use only a mild organic oil soap or neutral cleaner solution, and apply it sparingly with a sponge. (I use a wood oil soap that I had a chemical company formulate for me; you could also use one of the vegetable oil soaps on the market.) Then dry-buff it with a cleaning cloth, with the grain. If you dry with the grain, occasional streaks will never be noticed. A clean, dry surface on a paneled wall is much better than covering the paneling with "El Gunko" panel polish or cleaners that leave a sticky surface to collect and hold handprints and every passing particle of dirt and dust. The oil soap cleans the wood surface and leaves a nice shine.

Cleaning ceilings

Ceilings are always tough, even the easier-to-clean types like enamel, no texture or special finish of any kind. There is good news and bad news for you women who for years have had aching arms and back and neck from working above your head. The bad news first: A physiologist told me that the muscle structure of a woman's torso is built to transfer to her shoulders the weight of a child carried during pregnancy. When a woman works above her head, she's pulling against these muscles, so overhead work is much more difficult for her than it is for a man. The good news is: what an excuse to get a man to do the high work (such as ceilings)!

About 75 percent of ceilings don't need washing (ceiling washing is hard work, even for experienced experts). Use a dry sponge, and if a few flyspecks remain, dip a Q-Tip in white shoe polish and mask them. If a ceiling,

due to its texture, cigarette smoke stains, pole lamp scars, water leak stains, etc., poses a major cleaning chore, roll a coat of paint on. Ceilings are usually easier to paint than wash. If you try to wash (even doing it Aslett style) and you get streaks or "lap-over" lines, don't walk your new redwood plank—it probably isn't your fault.

Builders often leave textured ceilings unpainted in a new home. When five to seven years later the ceiling needs cleaning, it can't be washed because the texture (which is a water-based compound) will dissolve when water touches it. If you rolled one coat of latex paint on when the ceiling was new, it "filled" the texture and left the ceiling looking fantastic. But five years later when you try to wash it, the moisture gets to the compound (which turns brown when wet) and you have a streak. So always paint two coats on an unpainted ceiling and it will be sealed enough to clean.

When you do clean the ceiling, take down the light fixture lens plates first, pour cleaning solution on them, and let them soak in the sink while you clean the room. This keeps you from cutting your arms on them as you're cleaning the ceiling. Wash the ceiling the same way you wash walls. After you finish the room, use a cleaning cloth to wipe the loosened film and dirt from the plates. Rinse with hot water, dry, and put them back up immediately.

If you have either "cottage cheese" or those sparkly ceilings, your cleaning choices are limited. You can try vacuuming them with your extra-long hose and soft bristle attachment, or maybe you can dry-sponge them. You should also resolve never to hire any architect or contractor who uses the stuff.

Acoustical tile ceilings generally won't show dirt until it's too late to clean them. Clean annually with a dry sponge; it will only take a few minutes. If you fail to do so, you'll have no choice but to paint it. That ruins the looks *and* the acoustics.

Washing closets

I'd wash the inside of the closets once every twenty years or so; most of them are closed, so they don't get dirty. Closets generally take longer than the whole room, and besides, nobody ever sees them anyway. But when you paint your closets, use a hard-finish, light-colored enamel so they'll be easy to clean whenever you do wash them.

Don't forget the doors

Our doors get much more use than any other part of the house, yet we spend very little time keeping them clean and looking sharp. Doors are so taken for granted we seldom appreciate their contribution to a neat, attractive house.

I once gave my wife a rest and got the house in top shape. When I finished my cleaning marathon, for some reason the house still looked unfinished. When I looked everything over, I found the floor glistening, the walls clean, no dust anywhere—but the *doors* had marks from hands, scratches from carrying suitcases through, the bottoms had black marks from kicks, mop and vacuum bumps, etc.

Most of my doors are natural wood with a clear finish. Some are painted. The painted doors I cleaned with a soft nylon scrubbing sponge. If marks and nicks were present or the doors were dull, I simply repainted them. The natural wood I scrubbed with a good ammonia solution and a nylon pad. I cleaned with the grain of the wood and rinsed the cleaner off with a damp cloth. They were now clean, but a little dull. I made sure they were dry and with some extra-fine sandpaper, I again went over the door, lightly, with the grain. The sanding removed lint, dust, and hair particles that got in the previous coat of finish. I took a cloth dampened with mineral spirits (paint thinner and tack cloths work, too) and wiped the doors to get off every speck of lint and dust. (By the way, I left the doors on while doing all this and put cardboard under them to protect the rug/floor.)

I applied a coat of low-gloss varnish (you could also use a polyurethane finish) to each door (even on the tops), rolling it on so it was evenly distributed, and then brushing with the grain to prevent runs and misses. Then I just let them dry.

You won't believe the difference it will make in your doors' appearance and the ease of keeping them clean! It will take just a few hours and will help protect the doors from future abuse. Pick a day when the house is quiet—signs and warnings about keeping out of varnish aren't heeded. Do it on a dry summer day and the drying time will go fast. On a rainy day it can take 50 percent longer to dry. As soon as your bedroom door is dry enough to close, take a rest. You deserve it for all the time and money you have saved.

Remember—where there's a wall, there's a way!

15.

Painting without fainting

The construction company has just finished Betty Betterhouse's new home. Painting is all that's left to do before she can move in. The construction foreman put a beautiful texture on the living room ceiling, and some fine decorative masonry block work in the basement game room. Not wanting to mar the natural beauty of these surfaces, Betty asks that the painters not touch the living room ceiling, and has them apply just two light coats of paint to the masonry wall in the basement game room.

Betty moves in, and for two years she enjoys keeping the new home neat and clean. Gradually, she becomes frustrated with two areas in her house: the living room ceiling and the masonry wall. Some flyspecks, an erupting soft drink, and moving a pole lamp have left their marks on the pretty white textured ceiling. When Betty mixes some cleaning solution and tries to remove the blemishes, she is horrified at the results: When the liquid hits the ceiling, the texture dissolves and comes off. Although the texture had seemed to be as hard as concrete or plaster, it wasn't. The texture was composed of a water-soluble compound that, although it hardens, will soften again when it's wet. Betty touches up the marks with a little white shoe polish, but eventually she has only one alternative and that is to paint the ceiling.

One coat of an off-white latex paint covers the ceiling and it looks great, but its cleanability is still doubtful. One coat of paint is enough to prevent the texture from dissolving when it's washed, but streaks or lines will probably still occur because some moisture will penetrate the paint and react with the texture. As discussed in Chapter 14, Betty really should give the ceiling two or more coats of paint in order for it to be cleanable in the future.

The cinderblock walls in the basement receive their share of the recreation room residue and need to be cleaned. When Betty tries to wash the painted blocks, she finds it almost impossible to get the dirt out of the pits and joints common in masonry construction. Betty should stop washing and apply a coat of block filler, followed by one or two coats of semi-gloss enamel. The block filler will fill the remaining pits and rough spots in the wall and the semi-gloss leaves a good washable surface for the future.

Painting can reduce cleaning work up to 50 percent!

Fingerprints, marks, splatters, dirt . . . all will easily clean off painted surfaces.

When it won't clean up, looks bad, needs protection, or you just don't feel good about it . . .

PAINT IT!

Painting can be a powerful ally in your housecleaning efforts. I was a licensed paint contractor for several years and am convinced that a little painting wisdom can save you a considerable amount of cleaning woes and hundreds of hours of cleaning time.

Although books of "slick quick" painting tips have been peddled for years, they haven't convinced many homemakers that the task of painting a home, inside or out, is easy and fun. Painting is generally considered a dreaded necessity; it can, however, be rewarding for you, physically and emotionally, if you make it easy.

Almost anyone can be a good painter. The basic cause of the despair and discouragement of the home painter is that by the time you get fairly proficient in the task, it ends, and it's three or four years before you pick up the paint tools and start the learning process all over again. If you'd keep it up for a few weeks longer, you'd conquer most of the problem

areas and enjoy it. Don't fall for gimmicks, miracle tools, or "do-it-yourself magic paint," thinking they'll make painting easy. Basic painting equipment—brushes, rollers, and spray guns—can do it all, and in the long run, they're easier than the gimmicks once you learn how to use them.

Summing up all painting wisdom in one volume is unimaginable; doing it in one chapter of a housecleaning book is impossible, so I resort to some brief instruction.

Prepare before you paint

"Efficient" painting begins before you paint: preparing yourself, your furnishings, and the surface. The following suggestions will benefit all three of you. The mental anguish of mess and smell is what most people dread about painting. Minimize it!

1. **Clean**
If walls are very dusty, greasy, or dirty, you should clean them prior to painting, using a good strong ammonia solution that will quickly remove the dirt (don't worry about hurting the surface). Here is a place where the dry sponge can be a lifesaver. You can dry-sponge a bedroom down in minutes, then paint it. For other surfaces and problems, ask at your paint store—such service is part of the paint price. A rented pressure washer can have the exterior of a dirty house ready to go in hours.

2. Prepare

Use prepared spackle mix to patch holes. Pack the spackle tightly into the holes until it bulges (because it will shrink). Let it dry. After sanding it smooth, coat it with shellac to seal it. This will prevent dull spots in your paint job. As for nicks, bare wood, etc., always follow directions on the paint can. Use primer and *then* paint when surfaces require preconditioning—don't just use two coats of paint! A coat of primer undercoating is much better than a coat of paint as an undercoat.

3. Protect

Tromping through sheets of newspaper, half of them stuck to your feet with paint drops, while trying to untangle flimsy plastic dropcloths for your furniture will remove any doubts in your mind as to why Hitler was a painter and wallpaperer. Use old sheets to cover your furnishings and pick up a couple of 10x12- or 12x15-foot paint tarps—canvas or other heavy cloth—for floors. Hard paint droplets won't chip off cloth like they do off plastic. Cloths and tarps aren't expensive, will last for years, and you'll find many other uses for them.

4. Ventilate

For some reason most people think that heat is what's needed to dry things. Wrong. It's air circulation that does most of the drying. Cool air circulating freely will dry paint faster than a sealed house with the heat up to 80°. Breathing paint fumes can be physically harmful as well as discouraging. Get plenty of air flow—it helps you and the paint!

Remember that pregnant women shouldn't *ever* paint, or even be around paint fumes.

Use the right paint

If you use a top-grade washable paint, you won't have to paint as often. Handprints, flyspecks, food or splashes, hair oil, etc., penetrate into flat paint and often cannot be removed. Use enamel paint for more efficient cleaning. I like satin enamel for surfaces that will be abused. Latex enamels are great; just make sure you prime the surface if you're painting over old oil paint, or it will chip on you if you don't.

Buy well-known, high-quality brands. Good paint goes further, covers better, and lasts longer than the bargain cheapies. The extra $5 spent on a gallon of paint is one of the best cleaning investments you'll ever make.

Select a "reasonable" color. Use as much of the same color throughout your home as possible. Too many homes look like an Easter basket because homemakers are still trying to decorate their homes with paint. The color and style of modern furniture, drapes, and carpet do a fine job of giving a home richness and taste. Using a single soft off-white shade on all the walls, ceilings, and woodwork will allow your furnishings to flatter your home and will simplify your painting because it won't go out of style. (And all your touch-up paint is in one can.)

Choosing the room color from a color chip has caused many a nervous collapse after the paint is on. Paint is always darker and brighter than you expected when you looked at the chip. When you get the shade and color you think you want, move a couple of shades lighter on the color chart. You'll probably be much happier with the results. Besides, lighter colors are more cheerful, reduce lighting costs, and simply look and feel cleaner.

Buy professional paint equipment and take care of it

Most paint stores carry professional equipment. Selecting the right equipment isn't really difficult—just stay away from the 69¢ throwaway brushes and rollers. Good brushes and heavy-duty rollers will cover better, apply faster and more evenly. Ask the dealer where the professional lines are and select a nylon bristle brush; nylon lasts and keeps its spring. An angled sash brush will do a lot for your aim on trim.

I use a thick roller cover on most jobs—3/8- to 1/2-inch pile—because it holds more paint and covers more thoroughly. (Most dealers, though, will tell you "thin for bare walls, thick for deep texture.") All rollers leave an orange-peel effect (which I like; if you don't you can lightly run a brush over it when you're finished and have a smoother, glossier job). Learn to use roller extension handles. They work beautifully with professional rollers and are much safer, more effective, and less tiring than painting from a ladder. A two-foot effort with your arms will project a six-foot effort on the painting surface. Using extension handles will be awkward at first, but they're faster than holding a roller frame in your hand. (They also get you back from your work so you can see what you're doing.)

Buy good equipment

Buy a good grade of paint. Most of your work—and cost—is in the preparation for painting. The little more you spend on a good-quality paint will cover the surface faster and better, look better, and make all that hard work last much longer!

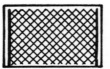

Invest in a professional roller frame with an extension handle.

Buy professional-quality roller covers with 3/8"-1/2" nap.

A roller screen and

a 5-gallon plastic bucket are an inexpensive, effective, and easy combination to use.

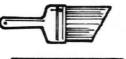

Buy professional-quality brushes. Nylon bristles last and hold their "spring."

An angled sash brush will aid your trimming accuracy.

Get ample free paint sticks.

This is one place rags come in handy.

A deeper roller pan or a bucket with screen will boost your efficiency and lessen the possibility of spills. Pick up a free 5-gallon plastic bucket somewhere (the kind dry-walling compound, bulk peanut butter, etc., come in) and get a roller screen for it. They're quick, safe, and easy to use. When you're at the paint store, be sure to get enough free paint sticks.

Don't forget to use your plank, ladder, and box combination, too. They will make your painting task a lot easier.

Some tips on technique

● *Prevent drips*

Punching a hole with a nail in the inside lip gutter of the can will eliminate "can run."

When you first open the paint bucket, use an awl, punch, or nail and punch several holes inside the lid groove. All the excess paint that used to run down the side will run back into the bucket and when the lid goes on, it will seal tight without squirting paint all over the side or all over you.

● *Proper thinning may help your paint job*

Solvent evaporation causes many enamel paints to get "heavy" when stored or while in use. Thin it down! Getting paint or varnish to a flowing consistency will create a brushed or rolled surface as smooth as silk. Use a recommended thinner (not gasoline or other substitutes) for oil-based or resinous paints; water for latex, of course! Go slow—if you get it too thin, you can't thicken it. Letting paint run off a dipped stir stick is a good way to judge consistency. If enamel runs to a point two inches below the stick before it breaks into droplets, it's just right.

If your paint or varnish looks too thin as soon as you open the can, insufficient stirring is the most probable cause—the heavy pigments are likely to have settled on the bottom. Always have the paint store shake the can on their machine. It's much easier and safer—the lid could come off while you're shaking it.

People tend not to stir varnish enough. Because it's clear, it looks mixed and fools the user. Varnish "driers" settle out on the bottom, and if not stirred well, varnish will take forever to dry!

● *Most people paint too heavily*

When you do that, the sharp, crisp trim edges and corners become so gobbed they make the house look cheap and sloppy (and you can hardly tell the trim from the wall). Any damage to the surface, which happens in even the best-kept homes, is deep and ugly and almost impossible to blend in when the surface is recoated.

● *Prevent a dripping brush*

Dip the bristles just halfway into the paint; then, holding the brush flat, wipe the back side and bottom of the brush across the bucket rim.

● *Always drag the last stroke of the brush into the finished area*

Don't pull it away. If you brush into the finished area, there won't be a brush mark.

● *Roll properly*

Even though you've rolled over a surface once and it appears covered, it isn't. Cross over it three or more times for a good-looking, well-distributed paint job. The first roller pass appears adequate, but small "pinholes" or air holes are there that won't show until the paint is dry. Always roll in an up-and-down pattern.

Trimming the fuzzy edges of the roller will help minimize roller lines.

● *Paint in this order:*

When painting a room, trim around the ceiling and woodwork first, so that the paint you roll on later will lap over the trimmed edges and they won't show (use the paint can as a "trim bucket" so you can avoid the inconvenience of dipping a brush into a roller pan). Roller-paint walls next. Dip the roller in the paint, roll off the excess on the screen, then apply it to the wall, always going up on the first stroke so paint won't puddle down. Paint woodwork last, preferably with a semi-gloss enamel. Always do the baseboards last of all, because your brush (and paint) will pick up all kinds of hair and lint from the carpet or floor.

Cleanup

The most dreaded part of painting won't be a chore at all if you always scrape the paint out of the roller before you try to wash or clean it out. Use the curve in the handle of the paint stick or the side of a putty knife for this messy job. Some rollers can hold about a cup of paint, and leaving it in results in a waste of paint, solvent, and cleaning time. If you don't scrape it, you can wash it, squeeze it, and never seem to get anywhere—paint will come out of rollers forever. If you've scraped it properly, you can clean a roller in minutes with a small amount of thinner or water.

Once the roller is scraped dry, place it in an empty pan or bucket with a few cups of thinner, squeezing and massaging with your hands to loosen

the remaining paint. Repeat until the solvent comes out clean, then spin the roller vigorously on a pole or post (or your arm, if you're desperate). Centrifugal force will throw the moisture effectively out of the nap. Rollers and brushes used in latex paints are most easily cleaned under a stream of running water, either in the sink or outside with a hose.

Get all the paint you can out of a brush before cleaning by wiping it on the inside edge of the bucket or by painting it dry. Dip it in the solvent and swish it around to release (dissolve) the paint on the bristles. Again, a quick spin between your palms will accomplish more than ten minutes of sloshing. When the brush doesn't cloud the thinner, it's clean. A couple of tablespoons of vegetable oil on the brush will preserve and soften it if its next use is a long way off. When finished, seal the brush in aluminum foil or plastic wrap; the oil can be wiped off with a rag when you use it again for enamel, but it should be washed with soap and water prior to use with latex.

Always keep leftover paint for touch-up. Seal it well, and label it. Small glass jars with tight-fitting lids make fine touch-up containers.

Roller cleanup

A roller can hold up to a cup of paint. Before cleaning, always scrape a roller with the groove in the handle of the paint stick.

When you're finished cleaning it, always take the roller off the frame and let it dry.

Brush cleanup

Pour paint thinner or water in a bucket and let the brush soak a bit.

Agitate up and down and around. Repeat if traces of paint remain in the solvent.

Then spin the brush dry. Repeat.

Wallpaper removal

In my first fifteen years of cleaning contracting, I did an enormous amount of wallpaper removing. You might like to know in a few sentences what it took me fifteen years to learn.

If you can avoid removing wallpaper, make every effort to do so. But if you can't, then I would recommend the following: First, you'll waste your time and money getting steamers, magic wallpaper paste dissolvers, torture boards with nails in them, and other gimmickry. I stewed and sweated with all of them for hundreds of hours, thinking something must be wrong with me. (Little did I know that everyone who uses these has the same results and the same paranoia about their efforts.) With all of their "magic," and five helpers, the lady of the house and I would end up with putty chisels or knives, picking, gouging, and scraping off scraps of wallpaper.

The best thing to do is to get a bucket of warm water and a big sponge. Set up your plank so that you can get at the entire surface you want removed. Then wet one end of the area down as heavily as possible (just so it doesn't run down the wall too much). Cover the entire area, then go back and start over again, again, and again. It really isn't much work, it's just boring, but keep wetting it. After about thirty minutes of wetting, check a place or two. If it's quite loose, pull the paper off; if not, keep wetting. Don't get anxious. If you wet it enough, the stuff will come off in a big sheet. Then wipe the soggy glue off the wall so it will be in good shape.

If wallpaper has ten coats of paint over it, you have four logical options: panel the wall, move, make it eleven coats of paint, or cover the wall with some sort of sheet rock texture compound. If both wallpaper and paint are still firmly attached to the wall—not peeling or "bubbling" off—this last is probably the best option if you want to combine good looks with ease.

If you don't want to be practical, however—if you really love that house, you really want the wallpaper off, and you're willing to suffer—that's when you get the boards with the nails in them. You need to scratch through those ten layers of paint to be able to wet down the paste on the wallpaper beneath them, because the whole trick is to get water underneath the paint. You might even want to add some paste dissolver to the water you're going to try to soak the wallpaper off with. But basically, after beating through that paint with the boards and nails, you keep wetting down the wall, and wetting down the wall, and wetting down the wall, and then you get scrapers and putty knives and start pulling pieces of it loose. There's no neat or pleasant way to do it, but it *can* be done.

Designing your own efficiency

I'm a firm believer in personal inspiration, and I believe that most of the time *you* can figure things out better and quicker than "Dr. Home Advice" can in his column or book. When you meet a problem that's unique to you, nothing is more rewarding than using your own ability to zero in on it and solve it. You say you hate to paint the inside of the cupboards? Pick up your big furry cat and the neighbor's shaggy dog, dip them in a roller pan of paint, throw them both inside the cupboard, close the door, and if a fight doesn't immediately ensue, beat a little war rhythm on the side of the cupboard with your fists. The stimulated animals will evenly and expertly distribute the paint on the inside surface, and all you'll have to do is touch up a few tracks and give the animals a bath.

Obviously, you're not going to do this, but what I'm trying to say is that nothing is impossible. Don't think negatively—and don't restrict your thinking when you're trying to solve a problem. Your personal ingenuity is limitless! Everyone reading this book has had from one to a hundred ideas that he or she was going to build into a dream home to save housework. Most of these ideas were brilliant in concept, workable, economical, practical, and capable of saving hundreds, even thousands of hours of household toil.

But though they came from the best source in the world, the homemaker, not even a minute percentage of these ideas have been developed. The excitement of that special timesaving idea was lost in the hassle of satisfying financial, federal, and other bureaucrats who can't bring themselves to grant loans for "weirdo ideas." Enthusiasm was dampened by the blank stare on the contractor's face or the hesitation as the bank officer cleared his throat. Thus people end up taking what they can get—an ordinary old house crowded with things that require maintenance time the rest of their lives. Most homeowners are still hoping that some resourceful, pioneering young architect will major in designing chore-free homes and

liberate us all with one grand swoop of the drafting pen. Well, so far it hasn't happened, and you can rest assured that it won't happen . . . at least not in that way. The homemaker should spark such a revolution. Will the homemaker respond? I hope so.

Again, it all boils down to how valuable your time is. Work can be lessened, and time saved, by sensible maintenance planning and decorating. For example, bathrooms bedecked with velvet Kleenex covers, Tiffany lamps, knickknack shelves, and a couple of your favorite watercolor paintings will be a drain to maintain unless you have limitless hours to clean or you have an outhouse fixation. A bathroom is no place for elaborate artwork, oriental carpets, or other hard-to-maintain furniture and fixtures. Keep in mind the following:

1. Will it clean?

2. Will it last?

3. Is it usable?

If you weigh these questions carefully, it will save you a lot of hours cleaning hand-carved toilet paper holders and towel racks.

Designing work out of your home is unquestionably the shortest path to household freedom. Whether you're living in a home, or planning to build or buy one, you can invent or install anything you want. If you're forever running outside your rambling ranch house to keep an eye on your children, go to an Army surplus store, pick up a used submarine periscope, and mount it in your kitchen instead of running in and out all the time. Just say, "Up scope," and scan the yard. (Ridiculous? Not so, if it works—and suits your needs.)

If you hate to clean around and dust furniture but do want to have large groups of people in your home on special occasions, dig a pit for a sunken front room and build in stationary padded furniture. I told you in Chapter 11 how we did it: Forty could sit comfortably and there wasn't a stick of

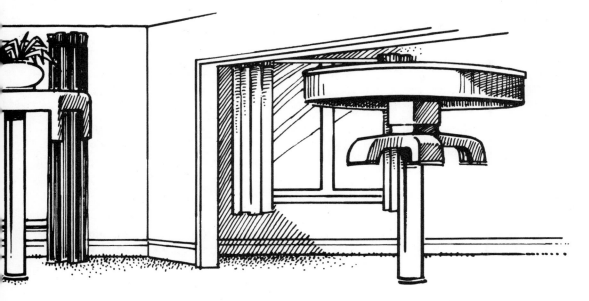

furniture to clean. If you've got husky children who are going to fight and wrestle, build their dresser into a stagecoach between two built-to-the-floor beds. Carpet the top of the dresser so they can play cowboys and roll down onto the bed. It will save a torn-up room and clean-up time, and besides, it'll be great sport for the kids. When they grow up and begin to act like humans, get them human beds! If you don't like to wash and paint walls, carpet them—they'll be a cinch to maintain.

If you are a short or tall family, hang your closet rods, paper towel holders, doorknobs, and mirrors where you don't have to tiptoe or stoop to reach them. If you run your home like a garage, put a drain in the center of the floor.

There are, in fact, six things you can do *today* to make your home easier to clean:

1. Eliminate it.

2. Hang it up.

3. Arrange it "right."

4. Make it simple.

5. Seal it (see page 80).

6. Remember that one is better than two, three, four, five, and so on.

Some time robbers to avoid:

● ***Indented or embossed tile or linoleum***

It looks great but recessed surfaces collect dirt, are hard to sweep, and will gradually fill with wax.

● ***Indoor-outdoor carpet***

It shows every crumb or speck of lint. It's difficult to clean and adds zero plushness to a home.

● ***Highly textured walls and ceilings***

They hold dirt and are a dust and cobweb paradise. They're hard to clean and paint.

Unfinished wood

Looks nice and rustic, but once it's soiled, you've had it. Wood should always be sealed with a resinous or polyurethane finish.

Fancy hardware

This takes time to keep up and provides breeding grounds for germs.

Extremely high ceilings

Although it's impressive to have a couple of 25- to 30-foot ceilings in your house, they're hard to maintain and energy-wasteful.

Multi-surface furniture and fixtures

Every surface needs maintenance—so the less surface the better. Eliminate ledges and edges where possible. A louvered door, for example, has much more surface than a simple, smooth door. Likewise, furnishings or walls made of many different materials take more time and types of equipment to clean.

Dark colors

Whether furniture, floors, or countertops, dark colors require more daily upkeep than medium-colored items (dark colors show dust and spots—everything!).

Decoration clusters

One nice big picture sure beats a clump of thirty-two dusty little ones (and cheats spiders out of bases).

Free-standing appliances

Washers, dryers, ovens, stoves, refrigerators, dishwashers: They have six sides to keep clean and the back and bottom are almost impossible. Most built-ins have one or two.

 ### *Carpet in high-risk areas*

It takes ten minutes to clean a jam sandwich from a carpeted kitchen floor—but only ten seconds off a hard-surfaced floor.

Windows in areas where you don't really need them

A window, because it's a light source, draws everything from flies to kids to animals to moisture. Window areas are high-maintenance areas, especially if they're complex or have drapes, shades, and curtains. Yet if windows are big, tinted, and unobstructed you'll spend much less time cleaning a windowed area than you will an equivalent stretch of wall.

You could continue this list for hours. Do so before you build or take over another house. Once you arrive at a timesaving idea and are sure that you want it, *do* it—not bullying your way, but checking and working it out with the builder, engineer, architect, or whoever is in charge. Remember, most people are chickenhearted when it comes to departing from the beaten track, and that includes many professional people.

On the other hand, a little timely professional advice may keep you out of trouble. For example, I designed all of the lights in our home to be wall-mounted 6½ feet from the floor. The purpose was to eliminate ladders and reduce physical damage to the house and safety risks in light bulb changing. It was a great plan. I picked out some handsome, expensive, frosted hexagonal fixtures and mounted them. We couldn't see a thing! Most wall lights, especially the frosted ones, aren't designed to shed light. I now have ninety individual light fixtures in my home and still can't see much without a candle or a miner's hat. A few minutes of professional advice would have showed me how to save forty of those light fixtures (and some expensive electrical bills) while getting better light.

Good design includes wise selection of paint, wall coverings, and carpets. Design, fix up, or build to fix your lifestyle, and you won't regret it!

You can come up with the details to fit your taste and energy level if you'll apply these maintenance-minded criteria:

1. ### Ease of maintenance
Once a surface is subjected to use, it will become soiled, worn, and dusty. A surface should be economical to clean (from both a time and money standpoint).

2. ### Accessibility
All surfaces, appliances, and decorations should be located for easy access. "Under," "up," "over," or "in back of" must be eliminated as much as possible.

3. ### Replaceability
Ruined or worn areas or items will have to be replaced some day. Working with standard sizes and styles will make this a lot easier.

4. ### Durability
Materials or structures must be able to resist wear from natural or human abuse.

5. ### Serviceability
Is the manpower or equipment to clean or repair the item conveniently available?

6. ### Safety
Is it safe?

P.S. *Make Your House Do the Housework,* an entire book on maintenance-free design, is my latest project (in partnership with my daughter), thanks to the response to this chapter in the first edition of this book. It will have hundreds of your ideas and a few of mine, as a professional cleaner and maintenance consultant, and Laura's, as a professional decorator and homemaker.

17.

Why not be a professional housecleaner?

Can you picture yourself next Monday morning? It's 9:00. All your housework is done. Your home is organized, and you're leaving it to go clean four other homes . . . for $10 or $20 an hour? No, it isn't a fantasy or a joke.

One of the biggest economic and social realities of the '80s is the two-career family. The effects of an extra job on family and marital relationships can be problematical. But that doesn't eliminate many families' growing need for a second income. Homemakers with or without children have flocked to the job market in an attempt to meet ever mounting inflation. In order to secure employment, many have found it necessary to purchase extra transportation, accept close to

minimum-wage jobs, hire expensive child care services, and spend a lot of money on a business wardrobe. Actual benefits from most homemakers' second jobs would be questionable if both direct and indirect costs were calculated.

Why go through the expense of all that overhead to gain a tiny percent of

income when you can double your profit for half the emotional and physical price you're paying? Why not start your own professional housecleaning business? It's not only possible, but will offer you some great personal and family advantages:

1. *Excellent income: $10 to $20 per hour for your time.*

2. *Tax deductions and depreciation breaks.*

3. *The potential for family involvement.*

4. *The ability to work on your own schedule.*

5. *Rewarding social and educational experiences.*

6. *Regular physical exercise.*

7. *Equipment to do all your own housecleaning.*

8. *Opportunity to pick your own working associates.*

9. *More control over your time and environment.*

Why get a job where you don't have time with your spouse or friends? Why have children you can't enjoy? Why fight traffic and parking and rigid schedules every day? Why answer to "bosses"? Why tolerate excessive deductions from your check? Why clear just a small amount of money for forty hours of hard work? On your own terms and at your own energy level, in your own selected environment, you could make the same money in half the hours and feel better physically and emotionally.

The market for housework is wide open. There isn't a household in America that doesn't need housework done—and most will hire it. Think of all the two-career families that desperately need help keeping the house clean. Franchised maid businesses are thriving!

Many struggling homemakers can't cope with their own housework, so that leaves the majority of your neighborhood or town needing help. You can provide it! There are lots of cleaning companies, but good professional housecleaning companies are hard to find.

If you are a woman, you have a number of advantages over a male in landing a professional housecleaning job. Homemakers are extremely particular as to whom they turn loose in their houses to clean, and you, another homemaker, will more easily win their trust. You'll love it, and it won't tax your personal life like a full-time job would. Though the image of being a "cleaner" and the hard work involved are big concerns to most potential scrubbing entrepreneurs, I assure you that handling the "image" is fun. And hard work will make you twice the person you are now!

The predominant fear most people have about trying their own business is, "Can I get customers?" This will never be a problem if you do high-quality work for an honest price. Even when I first started out, my success rate in getting the jobs that I bid was nine out of ten. Here are a few strategies that will help you.

If you just follow the directions in this book, you'll know more about housecleaning than anyone you'll ever work for. Every job will multiply your experience. You'll find that with your skills you can consistently average $8 to $12 per hour. Sometimes you'll get as high as $25 per hour on special jobs.

Regular everyday housework-type services (sweeping, vacuuming, dusting, etc.) are always in demand. But almost anyone can do that kind of housework, at about the same rate of speed, and this holds the worth of such jobs down. Try to specialize in the areas where the average homemaker struggles: floors, walls, window washing, rugs, etc. Competence in these areas will lead you to other, and even more lucrative jobs.

Getting started

The idea of getting started seems to cause even the most talented to shake in their boots. I know you can do it, and once you start, you'll look back, after the first three jobs, and laugh at yourself for being nervous about trying it. Visions of arming yourself with a mop bucket and dustcloth and parading up and down the streets beating on doors for business are out. You want to go to work, not jail! Here's a starting place. And don't be afraid to call people in the business (in other towns) for advice. They'll help you.

1. Get a name and a slogan

Just think—a chance to name your own company! Avoid personal names like Mabel's Cleaning, Betty's Broom Service, Jones Cleaners. Instead, use names like Century, Belair (like car names)—except relate it to homes. Such names have a ring of authority, and will inspire greater confidence. (Would you rather eat at Myrtle's Cafe or The Sea Galley?)

Just be sure you don't use someone else's name.

2. Have cards or leaflets printed

Always use a picture or visual symbol on your "advertising" literature of any kind. A bit of creativity, some rub-on lettering, some help from an artist, or a little free help from the printer will give you an inexpensive but effective tool to attract business. Avoid tacky "clip art" decorations. Be fresh and original. Your materials should be professional-looking and eye-catching.

Shop around for a good local printer and print 200-500 or more for the best cost breaks.

3. Check into the rules and regulations

Make a call to state, federal, and local tax offices and the telephone company and explain to them the scale on which you intend to operate. If you're just going to do an occasional job, with no employees, they'll probably say "no problem." But if you're going to operate on a large scale, hire a couple of neighbors, have a vehicle, etc., it's best to inform the agencies involved. The Yellow Pages, or your local Small Business Administration, will direct you to the right place to find rules and regulations. Explain your intention and regulatory agencies will generally send you everything you should know, free. They are fair, friendly, and will tell you exactly what's needed to operate a business. Don't get buffaloed by this part. It's easy, and the cost to you generally is little or nothing. "Acting dumb" to see what might happen seldom pays.

Check with your insurance company. The personal liability coverages you have now may also cover you and your little business, but check it out. Insurance companies don't cover workers or workmanship, only liability. If you fall through a window or rip a couch while washing the ceiling, you're covered under the liability section. However, if you break the window or rip the couch while working on it, *you* are responsible. Do arm yourself with the necessary insurance, but don't get caught up in morbid fears of what might happen. You'll have a few bad experiences, but be careful and conscientious and your victims will have great compassion.

4. Advertise

A business card pinned up in a laundromat or on a supermarket bulletin board may have some success but usually won't get you the kind of people you want to work for. If they can't afford a washing machine, they generally won't be able to afford you.

Classified ads in the newspaper are always good. Dropping cards off at local businesses gets both owners and clients. But the best advertising for housecleaning is unquestionably the personal referral. People who have their homes cleaned professionally love to brag about it, and if you do a good job, you'll never be able to handle the work that will flow in. A card or two

left at a house or a business you clean will quickly find its way into the hands of friends, and you'll find your way into another assignment. If your work is good (even if it's a little expensive), your business will boom and prosper.

5. Start small, and test it out

You'll be surprised what happens. One thing it will do is make your own housework easier and simpler.

6. Some of the best sources for work

(and reliable payment) are:
- Local personal residence cleaning
- Smoke-loss cleaning jobs for insurance companies

- Small medical or professional offices
- Construction cleanup, such as in new housing developments (be sure to get your money right away)

7. Some accounts to avoid:

- People moving out and away
- Shopping malls and supermarkets (there's often no clear-cut authority to make decisions or payment)
- "Maid" work for finicky folks

8. Hire cautiously

Wrapped up in the thrill and vanity of becoming a "big boss," you may discover a tendency to promise every ambitious or down-and-out friend a job. Be careful. You could end up working for *them* at no pay. Once your friends, relatives, or other job-needing associates go on a job with you, you may feel obligated to keep and use them on every job, even if they turn out to be worthless. You could end up spending all your time assigning, supervising, and cleaning up after them. Go slow. Start with yourself and a reliable helper and work up from there.

9. Get your own equipment

You wouldn't be very impressed if a high-class restaurant asked you to bring your own dishes, or if a surgeon asked you to furnish the scalpel. There is power and mystery in "professional equipment and supplies." They are dependable and deductible, as well as usable in your own home.

Don't go over your head on expensive specialty items if your business doesn't justify it. The equipment list in Chapter 5 should give you a good start. Put your name and emblem on all your equipment, for security and advertisement. You don't need a great deal of equipment, and you can store it in the garage and transport it in your car. If your business expands and you need a bigger vehicle, get a van. You don't need a $20,000 fur-lined van. One three to ten years old is fine because you won't be driving it that much—maybe a couple of miles, and then it's parked for hours while you clean a house. There's no sense carrying the insurance, interest, and overhead on an expensive new one, because you'll probably only put 5,000 or fewer miles a year on the vehicle, as most of your work will be close to you. Paint your van white or a bright color and letter it; it will be great advertising. Don't let your family use it to go fishing or haul firewood or hot-rod around in. Have a few simple shelves built into it, and install curtains if there are any windows. The curtains will serve two purposes: They make the van look more homey, and they reduce temptation to thieves.

10. Involve the family

These days there aren't enough paper routes or grocery store bagging jobs to go around. Once you get clients who love and trust you, they will need other services such as painting, grass cutting, and yard work. This is a natural for your children while you clean the house. Imagine your spouse cleaning the fireplace or toilet bowl under your strict supervision. (It will probably never happen, but it's a great thought anyway.)

11. Fill your work list and time schedule

Having a small housecleaning business isn't going to give you an ulcer. The fact that you book your own clients leaves you the master. You have the freedom to work just a couple of hours a week—or eighty, if you have the energy. Everyone's family and social obligations are as unique as his or her physical stamina and emotional needs. If all your children are in school, then you'll have three hours in the morning and three in the afternoon. You could work all week or once a week. Many businesses like their cleaning done from four to six a.m., and if you're a nervous-energy type like me, that's a good time.

You're the captain of your own ship; you decide when, where, and how. If you can't conform to a client's wishes, or bend enough to meet them, don't bother; they can get someone else. The reason you got into the business was to run it your way, not to let it run you.

12. Learn to bid your work

Don't work by the hour! Everybody in the world thinks a "cleaning lady" should get a few bucks an hour. If you quoted $5 an hour to wash someone's windows she'd gasp unbelievingly at your nerve, even if you told her it would only take three hours ($15). However, if you said, as you wrote the price on your card and handed it to the homemaker, "I have looked at your windows carefully and feel that considering labor, materials, and equipment, I can do them for $30," she would nod gratefully. Most customers find that a set price is more acceptable than a per-hour rate. Plus it's a relaxed situation—they know what it's going to cost.

The most-asked question in the industry is "How do I know how much to bid?" That's easy: Figure how long it will take you and multiply by what you want to make an hour. The better and faster you become, the more you have to charge. After a few months, you'll know your actual production time and will be able to estimate closely. You'll over- or under-estimate a few times (you might have to work free a few times)—and you'll learn from it. But once you get good, your confidence will "wax" strong, and you'll get almost every job you bid. This little table of average professional costs will give you some guidance in getting started.

Remember, this table is only a guide. You'll be able to plug your own figures in after a little experience. Who you work for as well as the quality of home and furnishings you're working on will make a lot of difference in the amount of cleaning time required. Much depends on the total area, size of rooms, type of paint on the walls (enamel or flat), the density of furnishings, who furnishes the equipment, whether you or they get the area ready, the level of previous maintenance, how far you have to travel, etc. You'll have a few losses, but that will stimulate your desire to be more accurate and you'll get good!

Always bid work. This is the basic formula for success in your own business. On a bid job, you can earn twice as much money by the hour if you work twice as hard.

But unless the customer demands it, or the job is very small, never give a bid price at the time you go to look at a job. Leave the customer convinced that you're the best-qualified person for the job and that she'll be missing out if she doesn't have you do the work. (Brag on yourself a little.)

Bid Estimate Guide

Walls and ceilings Cleaning	per sq. ft.	small room	medium room	large room
Hall	3¢	$ 7	$10	$12
Den	3¢	11	16	20
Recreation room	3¢	18	25	30
Living room	3-4¢	18	26	36
Dining room	3-4¢	12	16	18
Bedroom	3-4¢	10	15	21
Entrance	4¢	5	8	13
Bathroom	4¢	5	8	12
Kitchen	4-5¢	14	25	35
Stair landing	5¢	12	14	20
Utility room	5¢	10	12	14

Hard-surfaced floors	lightly soiled	average	filthy
Clean	1 ¢ (per sq. ft.)	2¢ (per sq. ft.)	3¢ (per sq. ft.)
Clean and wax	3¢ "	5¢ "	7¢ "
Strip and wax	8¢ "	10¢ "	12¢ "

Carpets

Vacuum and spot-clean	1 ¢ "	2¢ "	3¢ "
Spin-surface	3 ¢ "	4¢ "	8¢ "
Shampoo and extract	8 ¢ "	10¢ "	12¢ "

Windows (both sides)

Small, accessible	3 ¢ "	3¢ "	4¢ "
Large, accessible	2 ¢ "	2¢ "	3¢ "
Small, inaccessible	4 ¢ "	4¢ "	5¢ "
Large, inaccessible	2.5¢ "	3¢ "	4¢ "

Upholstery	lightly soiled	average	filthy
Small chair	$ 2 (per item)	$ 3 (per item)	$ 5 (per item)
Large chair	5 "	7 "	8 "
Small couch	8 "	10 "	14 "
Large couch	12 "	15 "	22 "

Furniture
Clean and polish

Small end table	1 "	1.50 "	2 "
Average TV	2 "	2.50 "	3 "
Piano	4 "	4.75 "	5.25 "
Desks, dressers	3.50 "	4 "	5 "

Commercial Janitorial *Square feet bid*	small office	medium office	large office
	5-8¢/sq. ft./ per month	5-6¢/sq. ft./ per month	4-5¢/sq. ft./ per month

Total cleaning production per hour	light cleaning	medium cleaning	heavy cleaning
	3000 sq. ft.	2800 sq. ft.	2000 sq. ft.

(total square footage quotes are of area actually cleaned or serviced)

Other business operation costs:
Vehicle—charge 25¢ a mile
Overhead—add 5% to your total bid to cover phone, advertising, etc.
Daily vacuuming, dusting, watering plants—$6-$6.50 per hour contract amount.

Return home, prepare the bid, and mail it to the customer. Handing the customer a bid and standing and waiting for a decision creates an unpleasant atmosphere. Especially with large expenditures at stake, the customer likes to study the bid and think it over before making a commitment. A commitment given in haste or under pressure often develops into a bad customer relationship and often affects the job and the promptness with which the bill will be paid.

The proper conversation while the job is being estimated can make a big difference. If you can see that money is a problem at the moment, and if you know that her credit is good, let a prospective customer know that you're agreeable to arranging suitable terms. (Compensate for this in the bid.) Remember, jobs you consider small or common may be great and expensive decisions for some customers. Take your time, examine the whole job, and add your personal touch to the negotiations. Don't be an estimator who deals only with square footage and not with people. The personal touch can be one of the biggest factors in whether or not you get the job.

Helpful techniques in preparing a bid

When preparing a bid, itemize and describe clearly the service you're going to provide. Picture words and specifics are much more effective than the bare minimum of information. For example, here are two ways a job could be described in a bid to paint a floor:

Example A
Painting porch floor, one coat gray enamel: $45.00

Example B
Preparation of complete rear porch floor area including light sanding, renailing protruding nails, removing all dust and foreign material, and applying one coat of Benjamin Moore Floor and Deck Enamel in Dover Gray color. Total cost: $44.50

Almost anyone would accept the second bid rather than the first because it appears to offer more for the money. "Preparation" is simply getting the area ready, and both bids include that. But example B *tells* the customer about it. "Light sanding" means removing paint blisters or scaly areas, and "re-nailing protruding nails" may take three or four minutes. "Removing all dust and foreign material" just means sweeping the floor. Example A didn't even bother to tell the customer that the floor would be swept. "Applying" is a professional word; "painting" is Tom Sawyer stuff. Professional-sounding words in your bid will help sell the job.

For large or long-term jobs, your bid should be submitted with a one-page standard contract agreement form (such as the one shown on page 164). Most office supply stores have them; your name can be stamped or printed on the blank form. Once a relationship of trust is established with a regular customer, a contract may not be necessary on every job.

Job Sheet

(for your records, and for invoicing one-time jobs)

Name _____ Phone _____

Address _____ Bus. Phone _____

Job scheduled for _____ 19 _____ A.M. _____ P.M. _____

ROOMS	CLEANING			PAINTING				RUGS	MISCELLANEOUS		
	Wall	Ceil.	W.W.	Wall	Ceil.	W.W.	Color#		Windows	Floors	Amount
Living											
Dining											
Kitchen											
Hall											
Bed											
Bed											
Bed											
Landing											
Entrance											
Recreation											
Utility											
Bath											
Bath											
Basement											
Den											

1. Total cleaning of walls—ceiling—woodwork	$	Cost $	Cost $	Cost $ Cost $
2. Total cleaning of carpets and rugs	$			
3. Total cleaning of floors and tile	$		Upholstery	
4. Total cleaning of contents—articles	$			
5. Total cleaning of upholstery	$		Couch	
6. Total cost of drape-cleaning & hanging	$		Couch	
7. Cost of windows	$		Chair	
8. Cost of repair or replacement	$		Chair	
9. Total cost of painting	$		Chair	
10.	$			
11.	$			
TOTAL COST OF BILL	$			

This proposal includes all costs of equipment, supplies, labor and other expenses needed to complete the job as outlined above. Any additional services performed over and above that which is outlined will be considered extra work and will result in additional cost. Your acceptance of this proposal as set forth herein will be indicated by your directing us to commence with the work described herein. We _____ shall be paid the sum of $ _____ for the work outlined herein. Work will be completed before any payment is made and work will be done wholly at our risk.

Authorized Signature _____

W-Wash   D-Dry Sponge   S-Shampoo   SW-Scrub & Wax   P-Paint

Tips of the trade

Here are some of my "Key Management Secrets for Successful Residential Cleaning." These are the small things that help get a job done—and a customer for life.

1. *Don't lend or rent out your equipment. Few people know how to care for professional equipment, and a lost or damaged part can cost you a month's profit.*

2. *When bidding a job, project the idea: "We are professionals who can and will take care of your problems."*

3. *Be careful about bidding or giving prices by phone. Type of paint, condition, location, accessibility, and the personality of the client can all create a bidding problem if you don't look over a job in person.*

4. *Show up at the house dressed for the occasion. A clean uniform always has a good psychological effect.*

5. *Carry crisp business cards, a new dry sponge, a clean notepad. Everybody likes to be the first one.*

6. *Tell the customer what will clean and what won't. Don't say "if" or "maybe."*

7. *Point out any damage or problem subtly, but don't criticize sloppy painting or construction—chances are they or their grandpa did it.*

8. *With urine stains and smells—dogs, kids, or other—advise the customer about permanent damage.*

9. *Look for more work as you go along. Mention it in a helpful way, without applying pressure. They'll appreciate it and gain confidence in you.*

10. *Always know beforehand who has the keys, how you'll get in and lock up, and who is authorized to be there.*

11. *Utilities: Will there be water? Light? Heat? Don't make any assumptions about this—it can cost you all the profit.*

12. *Volunteer to repair things (touch up nicks, refinish doors, etc.) if you can do so profitably. If they hired you to clean, it's certain they'll need other chores done around the house.*

13. *Even if the job you're doing is inside, ask about exterior cleanup.*

14. *Problem items: Some appliances can take longer to clean than a $30 room, yet charges of more than $5 will stagger the customer. Kitchen floors can be much the same problem. Be careful.*

15. *If you send a crew, always designate one person as "the boss" so the owner only needs to communicate with that person. If about every hour "the boss" makes quick rounds, nodding and grunting a few corrections and/or praises, the homeowner will feel greatly relieved that someone is in command and that he or she will not have to inspect. "The boss" should also sell future jobs while there.*

16. *Even though the job is done, always list in detail the operations performed; this makes customers feel good and helps get future jobs.*

17. *Always do some extras at no charge; after you've finished the job, casually point them out. If the owner finds a speck or two after you're gone, he or she will be less likely to call.*

18. *Always lock the house if you leave and no one is there.*

19. *Use professional forms for equipment, material, and operations.*

20. *Never, never arrive late.*

(Here is a brief contract we use for continuing accounts—maybe you could pattern yours after it.)

Maintenance Service Agreement

THIS AGREEMENT entered into on _____ between
_____ hereinafter referred to as
"company" and _____ hereinafter referred to as
"contractor."
Service address:

Contractors will furnish for the company building maintenance, supplies and services as outlined in the attached "Detailed Contract Work Schedule" which is made a part hereof by reference, in accordance with the conditions and specifications set forth in this agreement for a period of _____ months beginning _____ , 19____. At the end of twelve months of each year of anniversary date the agreement will be renewed following the negotiable review of specifications and terms of the agreement between company and contractor.

In consideration of the above, the company agrees to pay to the contractor $ _____ per month for outlined service plus other costs for additional services as agreed upon. Said sum shall be due and payable TEN DAYS after each of the preceding month's services have been rendered.

TERMS: It is mutually agreed that:

1. All work shall be performed by the contractor in a good and workmanlike manner, and the contractor shall also provide regular inspections by the contractor's supervisory personnel of all premises on which the services are provided to assure a high quality of work by contractor of services agreed upon in the Detailed Contract Work Schedule.

2. All persons employed by the contractor in the performance of services hereunder shall be under the sole and exclusive direction and control of the contractor.

3. All property brought onto the premises by contractor is owned by contractor and not subject to any lien or encumbrance resulting from any action of the company. The contractor may remove such property during any normal business hour at contractor's convenience without prejudice.

4. Contractor agrees to carry Contractor Liability Insurance for personal and property damage at the amounts required. Certificates of such insurance issued by the insuring carrier(s) shall be furnished upon request to the company. Contractor agrees to comply with the local compensation insurance regulations and to provide and pay all employee federal, state, and municipal taxes including, but not limited to, Social Security, unemployment, federal and state withholding and other taxes.

5. Company agrees to pay ONE AND ONE-HALF PERCENT (1½%) per month interest (18% annual percentage rate) charge on any past due accounts and agrees to pay any costs including reasonable attorney fees to enforce the provisions of this agreement.

6. Company agrees to hold the contractor harmless for any property damage claims in excess of $50,000.

7. In case of default by the company under this agreement, the contractor may proceed to collect amounts owing and/or take possession of all contractor-owned equipment. Additional terms:

8. In the event that the contractor continues to provide services on this contract beyond the initial term of this agreement and/or in the event of proceeding in bankruptcy against either of the parties, or if either party elects to terminate for any reason whatsoever, it is agreed that this contract will continue in effect until THIRTY DAYS after written notice of termination is given by either party. Notice is to be given in writing with proof of delivery.

9. Modification of this agreement may be made by mutual consent of the parties, which must be done in writing and attached hereto, dated and signed.

10. Company may, at its option, request the contractor to perform additional services beyond those listed on the attached detailed Contract Work Schedule. However, company agrees that any additional or extra work will be performed as per price specified at time of performance and in accordance with the terms of this agreement.

11. Company may not assign its right to this agreement without written consent from contractor.

12. Unless exempt under the rules and regulations of the Secretary of Labor or other proper authority, this contract is subject to applicable laws and executive orders relating to equal opportunity and nondiscrimination in employment. The parties hereto shall not discriminate in their employment practices against any person by reason of race, creed, color, sex or national origin and agree to comply with the provisions of said laws and orders to the extent applicable in the performance of work or furnishing of services, materials or supplies hereunder. No services will be performed which in contractor's opinion pose a safety hazard to contractor's employees.

13. It is the express intention of the parties that this agreement, its status, or form is at all times in the county of _____, state of _____, in which county and state all matters whether in contract or tort relating to the validity, construction, interpretation, and enforcement of this contract shall be determined.
Additional terms:

| _____ | _____ | _____ |
| Date | Agent for Company | Title |

| _____ | _____ | _____ |
| Date | Agent for Contractor | Title |

_____
Property Owner, if not same as Agent

If you need further information about materials, training, and professional journals, write to me, Don Aslett, % Professional Cleaning Source, Box 1692, Pocatello, ID 83204, and I can put you on to them!

18.

Your reward:
There **is** life after housework

Well, that's it. We've covered enough aspects of housework to provide a fresher, more realistic view of the subject. And until a robot is developed that can be programmed to do your housework for you, you'll find the methods and equipment outlined in the foregoing seventeen chapters to be the next best thing for getting the most work done in the least amount of time.

Don't come unglued if you discover that even after applying all the best methods of housecleaning and home management, you sometimes experience the mundane realities of the profession. Every job has them, and housework is no exception. So brace yourself, and take it with a smile, for you too are vulnerable to slipping vacuum belts, flyspecked windows, plugged drains, sticky floors, ring around the collar, muddy boots, tidal waves of dirty laundry, and five dozen cookies to bake for the Halloween party (on two hours' notice).

But you've made tremendous progress! You've learned how to clean house faster and better. You've also seen the error of the notion that everything to do with cleaning and housework is dull, unglamorous, and unrewarding.

I've been exposed to the same image you have of "the cleaner," and am still confronted with it every day. When I started my business while going to college, I received newspaper write-ups and a lot of publicity, and everyone admired my cleaning activities—as long as they were leading to something else. When I finished my schooling and still remained a cleaner, my social prestige diminished greatly. Several little incidents brought this to my attention.

One time I was doing a special job in a bank, cleaning the vault floors with a buffer. Customers were drifting in and out of the lobby, casting pitying glances, as they usually do, at the "janitor." At the time I had five children and was deeply involved in community affairs—I was a Scout leader and active churchman, I attended concerts and art shows, and thought I was riding the tide of social prestige along with the rest of upstanding society. One of the bank's customers was irritably dragging her loud and disobedient child along when suddenly in disgust she grabbed the

Maybe some day cleaning will be part of male fantasy.

little fellow, shook him violently, and, gesturing toward me, said, "Behave, you little snot, or you'll end up just like him!"

As the years have gone by, I've found that woman's opinion of cleaning people is nearly universal. Whenever I'm mingling socially and my community work or other accomplishments are described, some newcomer will always ask, "Well, what does he do for a living?" A hesitation and silence follows every time, because nobody wants to say, "He's a cleaning man."

People who meet me on the street and remember me from the early days because of the publicity my housecleaning business received will inevitably ask, "Well, how are you, Don? What are you doing now? Are you still a. . . ." They always hesitate because they can't bring themselves to say "housecleaner."

While she was at college, my daughter Laura skied at the nearby resorts whenever she and her friends got the chance. Since she had the car that could haul the most skis and

students, it was generally used as a taxi. After everyone was loaded in and they were off to the mountain, someone in all the chatter would always comment, "This is sure a nice car. What does your dad do for a living?" And Laura always answered cheerfully, "He's a janitor." The interior of the car would go silent for approximately three minutes, no one knowing what to say. Finally, in a politely patronizing voice, someone would say, "That's nice."

One of my managers, right after he was listed in *Who's Who in Technology Today in the U.S.A.*, was registering his wife at the hospital to have a baby. When the clerk asked him his occupation, he answered confidently, "Janitor." She looked up at him and said shyly, "Oh, come now. You don't really want me to put that down, do you?"

I could relate dozens of such stories, all hinging on the questionable status of being a "cleaning person." The image that society associates with cleaning—both in business and in the home—is totally incorrect.

I assure you, voting in a Senate chamber is no more important than cleaning a bed chamber! A glittering five-star restaurant has no more vital things take place in it than your ordinary, everyday kitchen. The home is the most sacred and exciting place on the face of the earth. For anyone to pronounce that caring for a home is a hardship, a drag, and a bore is only to admit a lack of imagination. Those who clean and care for a house, whether on a full-time basis or in addition to another career, can get great satisfaction from it.

Remember, though, that a house is to live in, not live for. Cleanliness is very important, but it should never become all-important. There is merit in being meticulous, in adding that extra touch of excellence to your efforts, but there is also room for caution here: Our zeal to achieve superior results can become slavish devotion to meaningless detail.

Homes are more than showcases and status symbols. Your home is the background against which your life is lived, your retreat from the world's buffetings. Why direct all your efforts toward impressing society? There's great fun and satisfaction in giving yourself to your surroundings, and in making your home a pleasing reflection

of your personality and interests. People will enjoy coming to your house, not because of its impressive trappings and expensive adornments, but because so much of YOU is there.

Personal freedom is life's real reward. Housework is an important and worthy endeavor, but the less of your life it requires, the more will be available for other pursuits that add dimension and joy and meaning to living. Housework may have become your responsibility, but it is not your destiny. Your real role in the home goes far beyond housework.

Pulpit, pedestal, or poetry cannot enrich the lives of others like a clean, happy, well-organized home life can. Humankind needs examples of order and confidence, and both of these virtues can be superbly exemplified in the home.

Children, and grown-ups too, need order in their lives. A feeling of contentment, comfort, and well-being grows out of neatness and order, not clutter and chaos. Self-esteem and achievement germinate in a quality environment, and no environment is more influential than the home. Our home atmosphere has a great influence on all of us—it can affect lives far more than any movie star, President, or professor. The spirit of our home can touch and change not only all those who enter and all who live there, but our own close personal relationships. It can make us irresistible as people . . . someone not just to be needed but loved and appreciated.

The home is the power lever of the world, and *you* control it.

Managing the home usually ends up being a woman's responsibility, not necessarily because she is a woman, but because no one else can or will do it as well. Some men think they can, but they can't.

If mechanics were all that was involved in homemaking, men might be as good at it as women are. But when it comes to bringing out the charm of a room, or adding the beauty and special warmth that make a clean home more than just a clean house . . . well, that transcends the realm of applied science or mechanics, and I'll admit without reservation . . . that usually takes a woman!

The good Lord knew what he was doing when he shoved men out into the world to plow the fields, sail the ships, operate the machines, and haggle in the business world. He knew that with brawn and a little brains, we men could be taught to handle those things.

But the home is where he needed the artists—the greatest concentration of intellect and sensitivity, creativity and devotion. It was the home front that needed the natural diplomats and the real multifaceted managers.

It is a delight and a marvel to see what a woman can do with a house. I'm continually in awe of a woman's ability to make things inviting with cheerful decorating ideas, imaginative color schemes, plants and flowers, and all the special little touches that have such a pleasant and positive influence upon our moods and sense.

In teaching, marriage counseling, and employing hundreds of people, I have found that women are special! On speaking assignments, for example, I've faced every size and type of audience imaginable, but every time I face an audience of women, I feel a great deal of warmth and compassion. It is real and it radiates from women, whereas it doesn't from men. Many a philosopher and psychologist has tried

to convince me that women are as mean, evil, scheming, and lazy as men, but I'm positive the philosophers and psychologists are wrong. I grew up in a good home, and my sister, mother, aunts, and grandmothers were all beautiful, positive people. I was eighteen before I ever heard a woman swear. The longer I live, the more apt I am to place a woman on a pedestal.

If you are not experiencing exhilaration from your role as a homemaker, it may be because your family has so much emotional and physical clutter that they can't reach each other to give love and appreciation. There is no greater goal or achievement on the face of the earth than the opportunity to love and in turn be loved. Thrashing around in the clutter of a home too often thwarts the opportunity to achieve this. Skilled, efficient house care will take fewer hours, fewer supplies, fewer repairs, prevent tension, and give us more room and a greater capacity to grow into new friendships and experiences. "First things first." *Living* is life . . . and we want to have as much of it as possible after housework!

You can save about 75 percent of the time, tools, and money you spend on cleaning if you will use the methods and materials the professionals do—and if you face the ultimate problem of housework, which is:

90 percent of housework is caused by men and children and

90 percent of the work is done by women. . . .

If they're old enough to MESS UP, they're old enough to CLEAN UP. Remember that your resources include your family's ability to pick up after themselves and otherwise help out.

What you used to see as the

thankless chores of housework might well be some of your greatest teaching moments. Think "teaching moment" the next time . . . you spend four hours preparing a lovely family dinner and end up with only a three-foot stack of dirty dishes . . . your sixteen hours spent sewing a satin drill team costume are rewarded with a whimper about the hemline . . . you proudly present a fat, tidy row of freshly ironed white shirts and he says, "Where's my blue one?" . . . you're on duty around the clock nursing the family through a siege of the flu, yet when it's your turn to collapse into a sickbed, there's not a soul around to nurse you . . . you know the kids are home by the trail of coats and books left in their wake . . . or by the jam and peanut butter and empty glasses covering the counter.

Remember, if you don't teach them, who will?

It's not a woman's job to clean, but tradition takes time to change. This book will be the best start you've ever had.

THERE IS LIFE AFTER HOUSEWORK!

About the Author

Don Aslett isn't just convinced that there is life after housework: He champions the belief that there is life everywhere every minute, and that everyone has a sacred obligation to take full advantage of it. Since his birth in a small town in southern Idaho, Don has pursued every channel of opportunity available to him. Teachers wrote on his grade-school report cards, "He intensely takes over and never runs out of energy." At age fifteen his parents taught and then assigned him to operate eighty acres of the family farm; he still found time to participate enthusiastically in high-school athletics, school government, and church and community projects. Don left the farm for college knowing how to work for the other guy, but found it unchallenging—and so launched his own career in cleaning, organizing a group of college students into a professional housecleaning and building maintenance company called Varsity Contractors.

But Don's first love, writing, was never dormant. Throughout the years of building a family and a business, he amassed volumes of notes on a unique variety of subject matter. Just a few years ago, he felt it time to begin to compile, publish, and market what he had written. In 1979, at the request of thousands of homemakers who wanted his housecleaning seminar information in writing, he wrote *Is There Life After Housework?;* the first edition alone sold half a million copies in the United States and England and was translated into German, Dutch, Swedish, and Hebrew. In 1982, Don followed with *Do I Dust or Vacuum First? (and 99 Other Nitty-Gritty Housecleaning Questions)*, and in 1984, *Clutter's Last Stand.*

Today, Don is chairman of the board of Varsity Contractors, a multimillion-dollar enterprise that now operates in twelve states. He is also owner of a maintenance consulting company whose prime client is the Bell System. Don is a popular youth speaker and leader, devoting much of his time to family, church, and scouting. He and his wife Barbara are building the world's first maintenance-free house in Kauai, Hawaii, but they still spend much of the year at the Idaho mountain ranch on which they raised their six children and numerous foster children—who now visit regularly with *their* children.

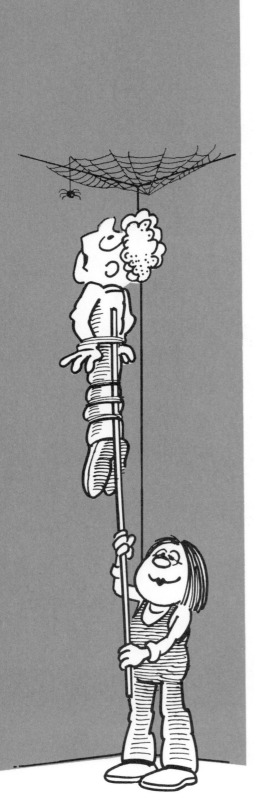

Acknowledgments

You know me by now, and you are probably well on your way toward putting housework in its place. But like housework, a book is not just one person's doing. The author throws all his ideas and energy into it, but a fine finished volume like this is the work of a team of people.

I'd like you to meet them, so that if you bump into them in Yellowstone Park or the Smithsonian, you'll recognize a few others who have helped to make housework easier.

The number one helper was *Gladys Allen*, a highly organized mother of many as well as a De-Junking engineer and entertainer. She beat out most of the male chauvinism that still lurked in my soul.

Next, attorney and member of my board of directors *John Preston Creer* forced me to sit down for a year and put my thoughts on paper.

Ernest Garrett first slashed the preaching and ego out of the draft.

Clark Carlile, my college speech teacher (and a successful publisher himself), forbade me ever to lose my humor and my "enthusiastic" style of expressing myself—he said it would go a long way toward making a book people might actually want to read.

Mark Lloyd Browning, one of the finest technical minds in the country and owner of a successful cleaning and maintenance firm, kept a keen eye on the "chemistry" in these pages and keeps me from killing any more canaries with ammonia (see p. 4).

Carol Cartaino, the all-time best editor in the world. (Gadfrey, would I hate to clean her house!) And her editorial tennis partner, Anita Buck, as well as the rest of the determined WDB team.

Judith Holmes Clarke, who first made me understand the importance of good visuals, and whose sprightly illustrations brought the first edition of this book to life.

David Lock, who brought his special impish touch to the illustrations of the British edition and gave us all inspiration for the next edition on these shores.

Craig LaGory, book designer and illustrator par excellence—who finally got a chance to do for *Life After Housework* what he did for *Clutter's Last Stand*. He kept coming up with good ideas and he kept his cool always, even when we said: "Her eyes are still too close together," or "The rags don't look raggedy enough yet". . . .

And of course my deepest thanks to you, the tens of thousands of you who have written and called and threatened to get the information you wanted. Anything we didn't get in this time, you may have to pray for. . . .

Index

A

Acoustical tile, 137
Advice columns, 41, 147
Aerosols
    vs. concentrate, 40
    limited use of, 39
Animals and cleanliness, 69
Appliance cleaning, basic rules of, 112-13. *See also under individual appliance name*

B

Bathroom
    bathtubs, cleaning methods of, 52-53
    cleaning, system of, 116-17
    mildew, 119
    sink, soap removal from, 50
    supplies and tools, 115-16
    toilets, cleaning, 117-19
Bed-making tips, 33
Blinds, cleaning of, 61

C

Carpet. *See also* Vacuums
    and anti-static agents, 95
    bathroom, 88
    care plan, 92-93
    cleaning, old wives' tale of, 35
    and cleaning spills, 100-102
    kitchen, 88
    quality and color of, 87
    shampooing, methods of, 95-99
    and soft vs. hard floors, 75, 76, 150
    and soil retardants, 94-95
    spot and stain removal (chart), 103-6
    and wear, 89
Ceilings, cleaning of, 136-37
Children and housework, 32-33
Chores, delegation of, 19
Cigarette smoke
    and cleaning, 128
    effect of, 69-70
Clean home, effects of, 169
Cleaning efficiency, 3, 19
    in bathrooms, 116-17
    and door mats, 65
    and waste containers, 68
Cleaning materials. *See also under specific household area*
    basic types of, 41
    chemical, use of, 51
    commercial exaggeration of, 7, 37, 107
    correct, importance of, 39
    homemade, 35-36
    and janitorial supply houses, 38
    location of, 53
    matching to job, 52
    window, 56
Cleaning methods. *See also under specific household area*
    basic principles of, 52
    commercial exaggeration of, 7
    professional, 3
    of spring vs. fall, 19, 35
    summary of, 72-73
Cleaning supplies. *See* Cleaning materials
Cleaning time
    list, 72
    decreasing, 35, 148-49
    and location of equipment, 53
    principle of, 49
    and proper equipment, 37, 39
Cleanliness, acceptable level of, 18
Closets, cleaning of, 21, 137
Clutter. *See* Junk
Concentrates
    vs. aerosols, 40-41
    types of, 41
Cooking efficiency, 13
Countertop surface, cleaning of, 49-50

D

Daily maintenance
    and floor protection, 83
    and vacuuming, 92
Directions, following, 41
Dishes, immediate cleaning of, 14-15
Dissolving agent, 52
Doorknobs, 119
Door mats
    advantages of, 64, 76, 85, 90
    maintenance of, 67
    minimizing cleaning time for, 64
    recommended types of, 66
    and types to avoid, 65
Doors, cleaning of, 137
Do Your Housework with a Hammer, 151
Drapes, care and cleaning of, 61
Dusting
    reducing need for, 111
    tools, 111
Dust mop, care of, 83-84

E Efficiency. *See* Cleaning efficiency
Energy level and production, 19
Equipment for cleaning. *See also under listing*
   for specific tool
   and cleaning cloth vs. rags, 129-30
   floors, 78, 79-80, 83-84
   location of, 53
   maintenance of, 36
   proper, 37
   storage of, 38
   where to buy, 38
   windows, 56-60

F Family, assigned tasks of, 33-34
Felt-tip marker, removal of, 14
Floor mats. *See* Door mats
Floors. *See also* Carpet
   care of, 82-85
   cleaning of, 50-51, 75, 76
   concrete, sealing of, 81
   hard, 75
   protection of, 75
   and safety, 75
   tile, 80
   wood, damp-mopping of, 84
Freezers. *See* Refrigerators and freezers
Furnace filter, change of, 111
Furniture
   design and style, 107-8
   fabric, care of, 108
   wood, dusting, 110-11
   wood, polish for, 109-10

G Gloves
   for oven cleaning, 113
   protective, storage of, 53

H Handbags, cleanliness of, 119
Hangers
   and household efficiency, 68
   and personal belongings, 33
Home, maintenance-free design of, 151
Homemade cleaning products, 35-36
Home maintenance tips (chart), 151
Homemaker vs. housewife, 5
Homes, second
   maintenance of, 21-22
   winterizing, 70
Housecleaner, beginning a career as, 4
Housecleaning. *See also* Professional
   housecleaning

organized approach to, 11-12
   and procrastination, 14
   system, 18-19
Household advice columns, 41, 147
Housekeeping
   and setting family standards, 32-33
   "up and down" style of, 18-19
Housework
   biggest problem of, 5
   caused by men, 170
   and children, 32-33
   first principle of, 8
   and husbands, 32-33
   methods and plans, 7
   minimizing, 3, 19
   and miracle formulas, tricks, 8
   and organization, 11
Husbands' share of housework, 32-33

J Janitorial supply houses, 38, 56
Junk
   accumulation of, 22-23, 24
   disposal or dispersal of, 23
   as relationship barrier, 25
   vs. treasure, 21

L Ladders
   alternatives to, 122-23
   and high areas, 125
   and plank, use of, 124
   and stair landing, 125
   use and basics of, 121-22
Light fixtures, purchasing of, 150-51
Lists
   assigning family jobs, 32-33
   chores, 12
   cleaning time, 72
   utilizing, 12-13
   value of, 16-17

M Magazine articles, saving, 22
Mildew. *See also* Stain removal, carpet (chart)
   bathroom, ridding of, 119
   prevention of, 70
Multiple-track organization, 13

O Organization
   to complete housework, 11
   household, 5-7
   by lists, 12. *See also* Lists
   of motivation and energy, 19

multiple-track, 13
myths of, 11-12
to run cleaning company, 4
single-track, 13, 14
Oven cleaning, 113

P Painting
vs. cleaning, 35
and cleanup, 144-45
equipment, 142
preparation for, 140-41
reasons for, 139-40
and selecting paint, 141-42
technique, tips on, 143-44
Paneling, cleaning of, 135-36
Personal belongings, responsibility for, 68
Plank. See Ladders
Plumbing fixtures, cleaning of, 19
Powdered cleansers, abrasion by, 52
Procrastination
problems created by, 14-16
vs. simplicity, 14
Professional housecleaning
advertising, 156
bid estimate guide for, 158-60
business, reasons for, 153-54
checking rules and regulations for, 155
choosing name of, 155
and equipment, 157
and hiring help, 157
job sheet, 161
sample Maintenance Service Agreement
for, 164-65
trade, tips of, 162-63
work sources for, 156-57

R Rags, 129
Refrigerators and freezers
cleaning, basic rules of, 112-13
top, cleaning of, 50

S Safety
and door mats, 65-66
and floors, 75
Schedules, set, 17
Scotchgard, 108
Screens, window, cleaning of, 61
Shower wall, cleaning of, 19
Single-track organization, 13, 14
Spray bottles, plastic, 40, 53, 117
Stain removal, carpet (chart), 102-5

Stair landing, 125
Storage
of Christmas trees, 23-24
strategy of, 25
of supplies, 38, 39
Storage-room organization, 24
Stove hoods and exhaust vents, 113
Stoves
cleaning methods for, 49, 113
spills, prevention of, 14
Sun Valley resort, 23
Supplies. See Cleaning materials

T Telephones, 119
Time robbers, avoidance of, 17, 149-50

U Upholstery, cleaning of, 112

V Vacation house, preparation of, 70
Vacuums
beater brush type, 89
care of, 90, 94
and fabric and vinyl upholstery, 112
and furniture dusting, 111
purchase of, 90-91
system, built-in, 92
wet-dry, 91
Vents. See Stove hoods and exhaust vents

W Wallpaper. See also Walls
painted, removal of, 145
removal of, 145
Walls
cleaning, basic principle of, 127
and cleaning cloth, 129-30
cleaning equipment used on, 131
cleaning, spots and marks, 134-35
dry-sponging, 127-28
enameled, 134
procedure for cleaning, 131-34
and rags, use of, 129
Waste containers, 68
Wax
application of, 80
need for, 75-76, 77
removal of, 50-51, 77-80
Windows
cleaning of, 54-60
high maintenance of, 150
Woodwork, cleaning of, 135. See also Walls

Learn more
about how to save housecleaning time and money with these other bestselling books by Don Aslett:

◄ **Do I Dust or Vacuum First?**— Don Aslett answers the 100 questions he's most often asked at his seminars and through the mail. Complete with charts, diagrams, and illustrations. 183 pages/$7.95, paperback

Clutter's Last Stand— In this ▶ "ultimate self-improvement book," Aslett shows you how to judge junk and select and store what you really should keep to help you get rid of clutter once and for all! 276 pages/$8.95, paperback

Make Your House Do the Housework— Aslett teams up with his interior-designer daughter Laura Aslett Simons to give you hundreds of exciting ways to redecorate, remodel, design, and build cleaning and maintenance ◄ out of your home. 202 pages/$9.95, paperback

Who Says It's a Woman's Job to Clean? ▶ — Aslett gets men to start doing their share of the housework with a quiz that helps them identify their problem areas, a "Housecleaning 101" mini-course, and lots of humorous, consciousness-raising illustrations! 112 pages/ $5.95, paperback

These books make great gifts for weddings, showers, or any special occasion, so use these coupons to order your copies today! Or use your Visa or MasterCard to order TOLL-FREE 1-800-543-4644 (outside Ohio).

Yes! Please rush me:

_____ Is There Life After Housework?, $7.95 ea. (#1455)
_____ Do I Dust or Vacuum First?, $7.95 ea. (#1214)
_____ Clutter's Last Stand, $8.95 ea. (#1122)
_____ Who Says It's a Woman's Job to Clean?, $5.95 ea. (#2444)
_____ Make Your House Do the Housework, $9.95 ea. (#1668)

(Please add $2.00 postage & handling for one book, 50¢ for each additional book. Ohio residents add 5½% sales tax.)

☐ Payment enclosed
☐ Please charge my: ☐ Visa ☐ MasterCard (Minimum credit card order $15)

Acct. #_____ Exp. Date _____

Signature _____

Name _____

Address _____

City _____ State _____ Zip _____

Send to: Writer's Digest Books
1507 Dana Avenue
Cincinnati, OH 45207

2006

Yes! Please rush me:

_____ Is There Life After Housework?, $7.95 ea. (#1455)
_____ Do I Dust or Vacuum First?, $7.95 ea. (#1214)
_____ Clutter's Last Stand, $8.95 ea. (#1122)
_____ Who Says It's a Woman's Job to Clean?, $5.95 ea. (#2444)
_____ Make Your House Do the Housework, $9.95 ea. (#1668)

(Please add $2.00 postage & handling for one book, 50¢ for each additional book. Ohio residents add 5½% sales tax.)

☐ Payment enclosed
☐ Please charge my: ☐ Visa ☐ MasterCard (Minimum credit card order $15)

Acct. #_____ Exp. Date _____

Signature _____

Name _____

Address _____

City _____ State _____ Zip _____

Send to: Writer's Digest Books
1507 Dana Avenue
Cincinnati, OH 45207

2006

For FREE information on:

☐ How to order professional cleaning supplies
☐ How to sponsor a Don Aslett Housecleaning Seminar/Workshop or speaking engagement in your area
☐ Don Aslett's schedule of appearances

Contact: Don Aslett, PO Box 39, Pocatello, Idaho 83204